Suzette's Alaskan Cooking

Taste Alaska Like Never Before!

Reviews

Imagine being caught In the Alaska wilderness with Suzette Lord Weldon. Not only would you survive—you'd gain five pounds in the process! You are holding no ordinary cookbook. This is an adventure in eating that is Alaskan in scale. Suzette has taken the best ingredients Alaska has to offer and given them her own unique twist. From the Salmon Potstickers to the Halibut Timbales, I can't wait to go fishing to enjoy these recipes. Compared to Suzette's Alaskan Cooking, *everything else is so lower 48!*

—John Tracy
President/CEO
Bradley-Reid & Associates
Former Alaska Television Anchor

Suzette has created a whole new excitement using our own Alaska harvest. Her recipes are positively mouth-watering and delicious.

In today's economy, it's a gift to have a cookbook that uses vegetables from our gardens, as well as fish from our waters, and meat from our land.

Striking just the right balance, the recipes are simple yet imaginative, short yet clearly explained.

—Bill and Donna Walker

For those of us that like to cook, Suzette has hit the nail on the head with her Alaskan cookbook!

She has taken our traditional foods and developed fabulous recipes that are true eye openers.

Her food is simply music to my mouth, and that's the wilderness way.

Thank you, little lady, I'm wild about it!

—Hobo Jim

Suzette's Alaskan Cooking

Taste Alaska Like Never Before!

Suzette Lord Weldon

Eagle River, Alaska

Photo Credits: Personal collection of author
Cover photo—Hank the Moose, Imageworks Productions, Roger and Moraya Davis

Art credits: Kimberly Bustillos

Cover Design: Vered R. Mares
Todd Commications, Anchorage, Alaska

Published by:

Northbooks
17050 N. Eagle River Loop Road, # 3
Eagle River, Alaska 99577
www.northbooks.com

Printed in the United States of America

ISBN 978-0-9815193-6-4

Library of Congress Control Number: 2010929588

Dedication

For my son Bobby and my daughter Desiree.
"Because I love them"

Other Books by Suzette Lord Weldon

Here's a cookbook for working folks who want to serve delicious dinners without spending all day in the kitchen. When your guests exclaim, "How did you do all this?" just smile and say, "I have a wonderful friend named Suzette."

Margie Bauman
Alaska Journal of Commerce

ISBN 978-0-9789766-3-7

Contents

Chapter 1—Farm Fresh Salads

Chapter 2—Sensational Seafood

Chapter 3—Wild Alaska Salmon

Contents

Chapter 4—Ocean Fresh Halibut

Chapter 5—Simple Suppers and Super Sides

Contents

Chapter 6—One Pot Meals

Chapter 7—Main Course Meals

Chapter 8—Delightful Desserts & Baked Goods

Contents

for camping

Foreword

We have had the pleasure of knowing Suzette Lord Weldon for the past several years as publishers of her first book, *Suzette's International Cooking*, and now this eagerly awaited book of her Alaskan recipes.

We have shared many enthusiastic stories, successes, and samplings of her delightful recipes every time we meet over the editing table and at book signings, where she dazzles the passers-by with a taste of her cooking along with sharing many chef secrets that have the visitors standing in line to hear her explanations. Many of these "secrets" are included in this book. She consistently is a top-seller at these shows and inspires her tablemate-authors with marketing subtleties that help them be successful too.

One of the unwritten ingredients in each of the recipes you will find in books is her enthusiasm and excitement for her creations. Read the introductions to the recipes where she gives personal examples of her experiences with each of the offerings, and you will get a feeling for this talent. Like any true artist, she cares for her creations like members of her family.

As you prepare any one of these recipes, you too will be swept up into the extra lift you get from sitting down at your dining room table, or around the campfire, eating and expounding to others about what your taste buds are experiencing.

—Ray and Jan Holmsen
Northbooks

Preface

People often ask me why I would move from the Napa Valley in California to Alaska. I always answer, "Why, the food, of course." In Napa we covet the wonderful sustainable foods from Alaska, like the wild salmon, ocean-fresh halibut, and the huge razor clams. The variety of seafood available in Alaska is so amazing!

So many new flavors and textures to explore! There are many different and intriguing kinds of berries. Take for instance, the watermelon berry; it's delicious and really does taste like watermelon, whereas the salmon berry, thankfully, does not taste like salmon but tastes like raspberries.

In the Mantanuska Valley our vegetables grow huge. At the 2009 State Fair in Palmer, Alaska, (which is in the Matanuska Valley) we had the Guiness world record of a 127-pound cabbage and an 82-pound rutabaga! The most amazing thing is that even when the produce is oversized, it is still very tender and delicious!

I love to fish, hunt, gather berries, dig clams, etc. My husband, John, and I take our Jeep and explore the wilderness. We forage for all kinds of flora and fauna, like juniper berries, which I love to use in some of my marinades.

I get a kick out of using what nature has to offer whenever I can. Sometimes I sizzle Tandoori Chicken on flat rocks, use alder sticks for kabob skewers, or cook our fresh-caught salmon on birch bark, which adds a lovely smoky sweetness to the salmon. Needless to say, we eat really well when we are on our adventures.

Living in Alaska has been a true blessing, a pleasure, and incredibly exciting. I have learned so much! I hope sharing my recipes will give you a taste of my Alaskan experience.

—Suzette Lord Weldon

Acknowledgments

—Special thanks to Kathy Towns for her time spent typing my cookbook and for being a great friend and recipe tester. And a special thanks to Calvin Towns for being the courier of paperwork back and forth.

—Special thanks to Jim Weldon and Alice Wittig for the time spent editing, proofreading, and typesetting my cookbook, taste-testing recipes, and for their support and praise.

—Special thanks to Kimberly Bustillos for her fantastic drawings for the chapter artwork.

—Thanks to Roger and Moraya Davis for the photo of myself and Hank the Moose.

—Thanks to my publisher, Ray and Jan Holmsen of Northbooks. Words can not express the respect I have for both of you.

—Special thanks to Suzy Walker who I think taste-tested most of the recipes in the cookbook and proofread them; whose friendship and encouragement means so much to me.

—Special thanks to my husband, John, for putting up with me being busy all the time and for believing in me.

—Special thanks to my mother, Lourdes, for instilling in me the passion and love for exotic foods from all over the world.

—Thanks to all my fans.

And in the sweetness of friendship let there be laughter,
and sharing of pleasures.

—The Prophet, Kahlil Gibran

Chapter 1
Farm Fresh Salads

Mat-Su Potato Salad

Sometimes I go out to a potato farm at Point MacKenzie and harvest my own potatoes, so fresh and tender that the skins wash off under the tap!

Ingredients:

5 strips of bacon, cooked and set aside
16 medium red potatoes cut into 2-inch chunks
5 celery stalks, chopped really small
1 medium onion, diced small
6 eggs
½ cup sweet or dill pickles, chopped small
½ cup mayonnaise
2 tablespoons spicy mustard
2 tablespoons grainy mustard
1 tablespoon freshly grated black pepper
½ teaspoon salt

Preparation:

In a large pot, put 6 inches of water and eggs and bring to a boil for 6 minutes. Remove eggs from pan and place them in a cold water bath, peel, and set aside for a few minutes until cool. Now put the potatoes into the pot and add enough water to cover, bringing them to a boil; cook for about 20 minutes or until fork tender. Let them cool.

In a large bowl put the cooled potatoes, celery, and onions. Grate the eggs, chop up the bacon, and put both into potato mixture. Add mayonnaise, mustards, salt and pepper, mix all together. Refrigerate until serving time.

Suggested Wine:

Riesling or Chablis

Neptune's Garden Salad

A feast for the eyes and the palate as well. Serves 4

Ingredients:

¾ pound crab meat, cleaned and cooked
¾ pound shrimp, peeled and cooked
4 eggs, hard boiled, cut into wedges
1 large head romaine lettuce, washed gently
1 jar white asparagus
½ cucumber, sliced
1 bell pepper, yellow, red or orange, sliced
2 medium ripe tomatoes; cut into wedges
Approximately 20 black olives
1 ripe avocado, sliced

Preparation:

Keep 4 large outer leaves from the romaine lettuce; set one on each of 4 plates. Chop the remaining lettuce and pile up on the leaf. Now start decorating the plates with the egg wedges, tomato wedges, cucumber slices, bell pepper slices, and olives. Then gently add the crab and shrimp. Make a cross with the asparagus on top. Carefully place slices of the avocado on the top. It should look wonderful and taste even better.

Serve with Blueberry Vinaigrette Dressing (p. 33).

Suggested Wine:

Chardonnay or Sauvignon Blanc

River Run Pasta Salad

When going on a river trip, I always take along a couple of salads. No matter how inclement the weather might be, it's always handy to have already-made comfort food. It's a whole meal in itself.

Ingredients:

Pasta rotelle or radiatori
⅓ cup onion, diced
1 cup snow peas, de-stringed and blanched*
½ cup black olives, sliced in half
1 small jar artichoke hearts, sliced in half
1 medium red bell pepper, cut into chunks
¼ pound cheddar cheese, cut into small cubes
¼ pound prosciutto or ham, cut into small cubes

Preparation:

Fill large pot with water, add ½ teaspoon salt, bring to a boil; add pasta, and cook for approximately 12 minutes, until al dente (just underdone); drain and cool.

In a large bowl, toss all the ingredients together. Add vinaigrette dressing, toss and chill.

Blueberry Vinaigrette Dressing (p. 33)

Suggested Wine:

Pinot Blanc or Riesling

---

*To blanch snow peas: drop into boiling water for 3 minutes, then remove and put into a cold-water bath.

Fresh Pea Salad

Fresh peas from the Matanuska Valley are famous throughout Alaska. They are so good. Serves approximately 6.

Ingredients:

4 pounds fresh peas, shelled
2 red bell peppers, diced small
1 can water chestnuts, diced small
1½ cups celery, diced
½ bunch green onions, sliced small
6 eggs, hard boiled, chopped fine
½ pound cheddar cheese, cubed small
1½ cups mayonnaise
3 tablespoons Dijon or Golden mustard
1 tablespoon Spike*
2 teaspoons dill weed, dried

Preparation:

Boil shelled peas for 5 minutes; using a strainer, rinse in cold water.

Mix all ingredients together well. Chill in the refrigerator until serving time.

Suggested Wine:

Chablis

---

*Spike can be found in your health food store or section of your local grocery store.

Spring Spinach Salad

Spring greens grow so fast here in the land of the midnight sun. This salad is oh so good!

Ingredients:

8 cups fresh young spinach leaves, washed and dried
1 avocado, diced
4 strips bacon, cooked and diced
2 hard boiled eggs, sliced into wedges
½ small purple onion, thinly sliced

Preparation:

Toss all the ingredients together, serve up in bowls. Drizzle with Zesty French Dressing.

Zesty French Dressing

I've kept this recipe a secret for 25 years. It is especially good on fresh spinach salad.

Ingredients:

1 cup vegetable oil
⅓ cup white vinegar
¼ cup ketchup
⅛ cup honey
2 teaspoons dry mustard
½ teaspoon pepper

Preparation:

Whisk together the ketchup and honey; add the rest of the ingredients one at a time. Adjust to your taste!

Suggested Wine:

Sauvignon Blanc or White Zinfandel

Tropical Dreams Coleslaw

We have a wonderful abundance of cabbage in Alaska. It grows huge, and I mean HUGE and delicious. So making coleslaw is a must-do. I have been making coleslaw for a very long time for catering jobs and family functions, and this is by far the favorite recipe with most people. Using the pineapple juice for the acid adds flavor without being too sour.

Ingredients:

5 cups shredded cabbage, thinly sliced (use some purple cabbage for color)
2 cups grated carrots
1 can pineapple chunks; cut the chunks in half, reserve the liquid
Or ½ can tropical fruit mix
¾ cup mayonnaise
⅓ cup raisins (optional) or dried cranberries (optional)
⅓ cup coconut, flaked (optional)

Preparation:

In a large bowl, toss the cabbage, carrots, fruit, mayonnaise; add ¼ cup of the juice. (If you want it creamier, just add a little more juice.) But before you add more juice, let it sit in the refrigerator to see if you like the consistency first. Raisins, dried cranberries, or coconut are optional.

Suggested Wine:

Chablis or White Zinfandel

Curried Halibut Salad

Great for sandwiches, salad, or stuffing into Pate Choux (crème puffs), or simply on crackers topped with Fruit Chutney in Suzette's International Cooking *(p. 81). I also use this recipe for chicken.*

Ingredients:

1½ pounds cooked halibut (de-boned) or chicken
½ cup onion, minced
⅓ cup celery, minced
1½ teaspoons fresh parsley, minced
2 teaspoons capers, minced (optional)
⅓ cup water chestnuts, minced (optional)
1 egg, hard boiled, minced (optional)
½ cup mayonnaise
3 tablespoons Dijon mustard
2 teaspoons curry powder

Preparation:

Break up the halibut into a medium-size bowl. Add the rest of the ingredients. Mix very well. Enjoy!

Pate Choux (p. 100).

Suggested Wine:

Riesling (off dry)

Roasted Beet, Purple Onion, and Mandarin Orange Salad

In the Matanuska Valley in Alaska, beets are another crop that can grow extra large. My neighbor brings me football-size ones. What amazes me is that they are still tender. I trim, wash, and wrap in foil. Bake at 350° F. until they are fork tender. Take them out of the oven and let cool. Peel by wiping the skin with a paper towel.

Ingredients:

1½ pounds or 3 softball-size beets, cooked, cooled, and peeled
½ small purple onion, sliced thinly
1 can mandarin orange slices, drained (reserve liquid)
4 tablespoons rice vinegar*

Preparation:

In a medium-size bowl, cut beets into bite-size slices or chunks. Add onions, rice vinegar, and 3 tablespoons reserved liquid, mix well. Add orange slices and toss gently as to not break the orange slices too much. Chill.

Keeps for about 5 days in the refrigerator.

Suggested Wine:

Chablis or Pinot Gris

---

*available in most markets

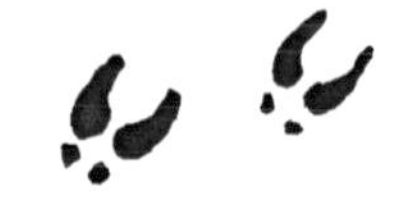

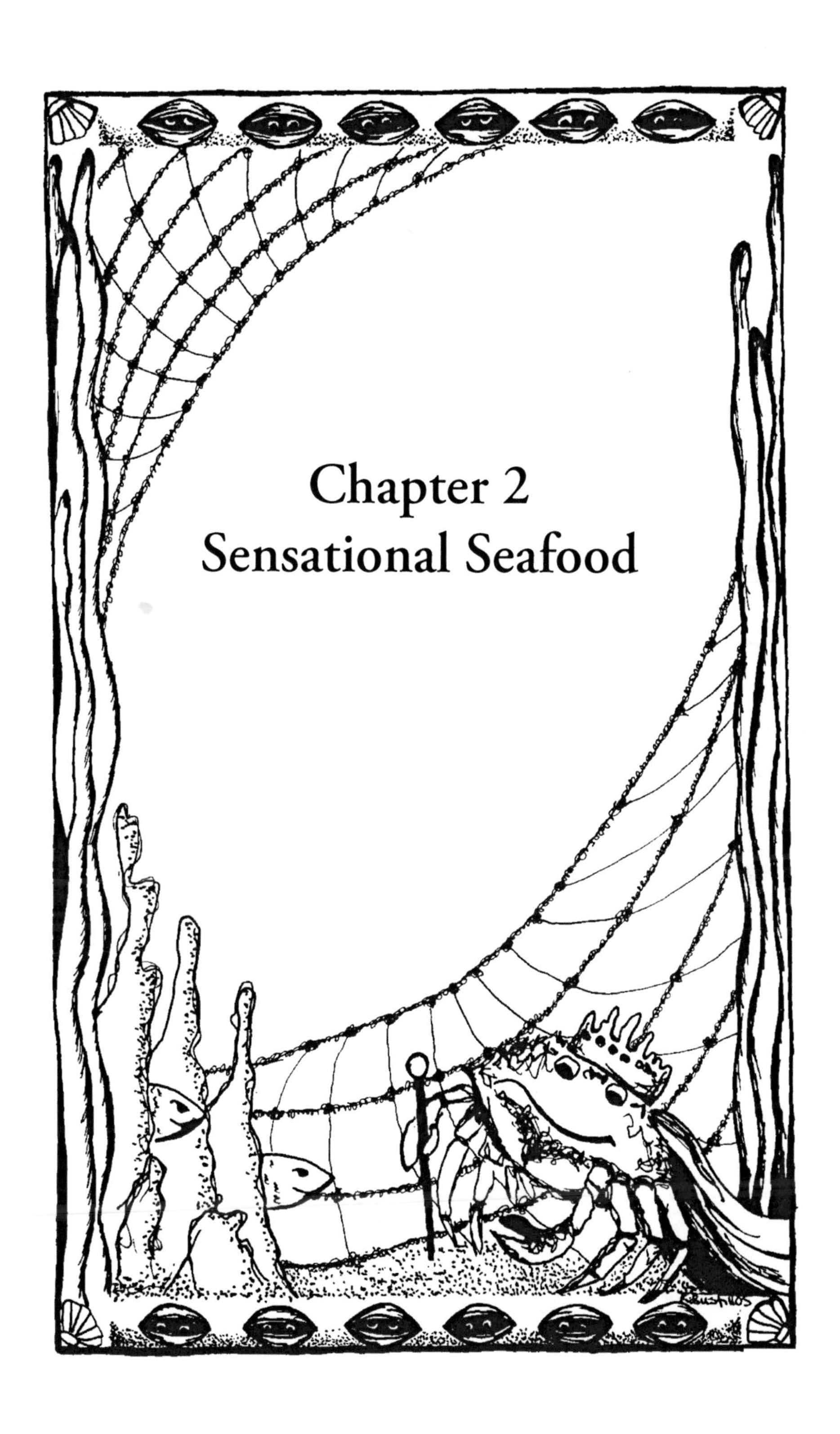

Chapter 2
Sensational Seafood

Alaskan King Crab Spring Rolls

You can substitute shrimp for the crab if you like. The dipping sauce is the final touch.

Ingredients

1 package spring roll wrappers
½ pound cooked crab, approximately 1- to 2-inch pieces
2 ounces bean thread vermicelli, soaked for 20 minutes in hot water
4 Chinese dried mushrooms, soaked for 20 minutes in hot water
1 tablespoon coriander leaves and stems, finely chopped
½ teaspoon garlic, chopped
2 ounces baby corn, finely chopped
1 small carrot, finely grated
1 cabbage leaf, finely chopped
4 ounces bean sprouts, chopped
½ pound cooked chicken or pork, finely minced
1 tablespoon fish sauce

Preparation:

Soak your spring roll wrappers in water until pliable and drain. Set spring roll wrappers aside.

Drain vermicelli and cut into 4-inch lengths. Drain mushrooms, remove stems, and chop caps finely. Mix mushrooms and vermicelli with the prepared veggies and meat. Add fish sauce and stir until well blended.

Open wrapper package and set the stack on an angle with a point directed towards you. Put 3 tablespoons of filling in the middle, then take the point closest to you and fold over the filing. Now fold each side in about 2 inches, roll up tight but not too tight, or they will break. Use a finger, dipped in water, to seal the edge.

Serve with Spring Roll Dipping Sauce.

Spring Roll Dipping Sauce

¼ cup water
1 teaspoon corn starch
2 tablespoons rice vinegar
2 cloves garlic (crushed and minced)
2 tablespoons sugar
1 teaspoon ketchup
2 tablespoons peanuts (chopped well)

Combine all ingredients except peanuts in a small saucepan and simmer 4 minutes, stirring, until sugar dissolves and mixture has thickened slightly. Cool, and add peanuts just before serving.

Suggested Wine:

Pinot Blanc or Champagne

Oysters or Clams Alaska

These are served on the half shell. This dish has always been a favorite of mine. It's a twist on an old classic, Clams Casino. This recipe can be used as an appetizer or an elegant entrée. If you want to make the clams, use little necks or cherry stones; they work the best.

Ingredients:

12 large oysters or 24 clams; make sure they are fresh and alive. Do not let the fishmonger close the plastic bag or they will die. Scrub the shells clean.
¼ pound pancetta, diced very small (if you cannot find pancetta, use bacon)
¼ cup butter
1½ cups bread crumbs (plain)
1 teaspoon garlic, minced
½ teaspoon Tabasco
½ teaspoon Worcestershire sauce
2 shallots, minced (or onion)
1 teaspoon parsley, minced
½ stalk celery, minced

Preheat oven to 350° F.

Preparation:

In a frying pan, cook pancetta until crisp, remove from pan and set aside. Remove all but 1- 2- teaspoons pancetta grease. Put into the same pan: celery, shallots and garlic, cook for 2–3 minutes. Now add the butter, Tabasco, Worcestershire sauce, and parsley. Sauté until butter melts. Add the bread crumbs to the mixture. Turn off the heat and fluff together.

Open the oysters or clams, discard the top shell. Top each oyster or clam with some bread crumb mixture. Put into a baking pan and bake for 15-20 minutes until golden brown.

Note: You can always steam the oysters or clams just until they open. Discard any that do not open.

Serve on a bed of rock salt so they do not tip over, or on a napkin spread on a plate.

Suggested Wine:

Chardonnay or Sauvignon Blanc

Mt. Redoubt Volcano Shrimp

Alaskan spotted shrimp are so delicious, but you can use any kind of shrimp you like!

Ingredients:

2 pounds shrimp or prawns, peeled (save the shells)
3 cups water
6 tablespoons vegetable oil
½ cup flour
½ cup butter
1 small onion, chopped
¼ cup green bell pepper, chopped

Seasoning Mix:

1 teaspoon salt
1 teaspoon white pepper
1 teaspoon black pepper
1 teaspoon cayenne pepper
1 teaspoon dried basil leaves
1 teaspoon thyme leaves

Preparation:

In a medium saucepan, add water and shrimp shells. Simmer for 15 minutes and set aside. Remove the shells, and discard. This makes a shrimp stock.

In a large heavy skillet, heat the oil until hot. Whisk in flour; stirring until smooth and an orange color; about 3 minutes. Slowly whisk in the shrimp stock. Whisk in butter and half the seasoning mixtures. Add onions and bell pepper, simmer for 10 minutes. Slowly add the shrimp and the rest of the seasoning mix. Simmer for 10 more minutes. Serve over a bed of fluffy rice.

Suggested Wine:

Chenin Blanc or Mourvèdre

Stuffed King Crab Legs

The trick in this recipe is to have a sharp pair of short scissors. Take the legs and see what side sits the flattest. Using the scissors, cut about ½- to ¾-inch wide strip all the way down, thus creating a canoe-like opening. Serves 4.

Ingredients:

8 king crab legs, approximately 2 large legs per person, cutting the legs as instructed, removing the meat. Roughly chop the meat and loosely put back into leg shells. Set all aside.
4 teaspoons butter, softened
½ cup parmesan cheese, grated
½ cup half and half
¼ teaspoon ground white pepper
Bread crumbs

Preheat oven to 350° F.

Preparation:

Mix all ingredients together, including crab meat. Evenly stuff back into the shells. Sprinkle with bread crumbs. Bake on a cookie sheet for 15 to 20 minutes until golden on top.

Suggested Wine:

Champagne or Chardonnay

Halibut, Shrimp, or Crab Tamales with Mole Verde

I started making these in my classes for a change of pace. I am extremely happy with the results, they're fabulous! Mole verde has peptis (pumpkin seeds) in it. A great recipe to make with friends. The dough and assembly instructions follow:

Tamale Filling Ingredients:

1½ pounds halibut, shrimp, or crab
2 tablespoons oil
1 medium onion, minced
2 tablespoons flour
1½ cups chicken broth
4 tablespoons mole verde*

Preparation:

Cook the seafood until tender. Chop into small pieces and set aside.

In a sauce pan, heat the oil and sauté the onion until translucent. Add the flour and the seafood and cook for 2 minutes. Add the chicken broth and mole verde sauce. Combine well and cook for 20 minutes.

Add a bit more broth if it's too dry. You want some sauce, but not too soupy.

Suggested Wine:

Sangria or Chablis

---

*available in your local grocery store.

Tamale Dough

One year I had four classes scheduled for January and February, and I ended up teaching eight classes! Everyone, it seems, wanted to learn to make tamales.

Ingredients:

2 cups Maseca* for tamales
2 cups lukewarm water or broth
1 teaspoon baking powder
½ teaspoon salt
⅔ cup vegetable shortening

Preparation:

Combine the masa, baking powder and salt in a bowl. Work in the water/broth using your fingers until a soft dough forms. In a small mixing bowl whip the shortening until fluffy. Add to the masa and beat until the dough forms a spongy texture.

Prepare the tamales with desired filling.

Yield: 16 small tamales

---

*Maseca Instant Corn Masa Mix is a product from Azteca Milling, available in your local grocery store.

Making Tamales

1. **Corn Husks** – purchased corn husks will be dry. To soften them for use, pour very hot water over them and let them soak for 30 minutes. Shake them well to rid them of excess water and pat dry.

2. **Assembling** – smear a thin coating of the tamale dough over the broadest part of the husk, allowing for turning down about 1½ inches from the bottom broad part of the leaf and about 3 inches at the pointed top. Spread the seafood mole verde down the middle of the dough. Overlap the sides of the husks loosely to allow the dough

to expand. Turn up the pointed end of the leaf and fold the broader end over it. Tear some of the husks lengthwise into narrow strips and use one for tying each tamale across the flap.

3. Cooking – fill the bottom of a steamer with water up to the level indicated and bring to a boil. Line the top of the steamer with corn husks, covering the bottom and sides. Stack the tamales upright. For best results, do not overpack, but pack in firmly. Cover tightly and allow to steam for 2½ hours over medium heat. Keep the water simmering, not boiling. To test for doneness, remove one from the center and one from the side and gently open them. The dough should be cooked throughout.

Crab Cakes

Alaskan king crab is so good! In this recipe, I took great care not to overwhelm the sweet flavors of the crab, but to enhance it. Other types of crab also work well.

Ingredients:

1½ pounds fresh, cooked Alaskan king crab meat, cleaned well and shelled
4 tablespoons minced onion
4 tablespoons minced celery
¼ teaspoon paprika
¼ teaspoon ground black pepper
1 dash (approximate) Worcestershire sauce
2 dashes (approximate) Tabasco sauce
3 large egg whites, beaten lightly
4 tablespoons flour
Bread crumbs for dusting
Vegetable oil for frying

Preparation:

Gently toss all ingredients together in a bowl except breadcrumbs and oil. With your hands slightly moistened, pat into 3- 4-inch round cakes. Sprinkle them with the breadcrumbs.

In a large frying pan add enough oil to cover about ¼ inch up the pan, turn on medium heat. Gently add the cakes to the oil for about 3 minutes on each side, until golden brown. Remove and place on paper towels.

Serve with a Remoulade Sauce (p. 41).

Suggested Wine:

Champagne

Seafood Kabobs 

So many different combinations work well. They are easy to make and fun to eat! The trick is to cut approximately the same-size pieces of all the ingredients so they cook evenly. Always soak your wooden cooking skewers in water; the metal ones work well also. Here are a couple of my favorite pairings.

1. Shrimp, scallops and cherry tomatoes, alternate on skewer.

2. Halibut and salmon–large chunks–lemon wedges and onions, alternate on skewer.

Season your kabobs with salt and pepper and a little olive oil. Grill indoors on a grill pan, or outdoors on the barbeque grill on medium heat. It takes about 20-30 minutes, depending on the thickness of the chunks of fish. Shrimp and Scallops take less time; cook approximately 5 minutes on each side.

Suggested Wine:

Sauvignon Blanc or Chenin Blanc

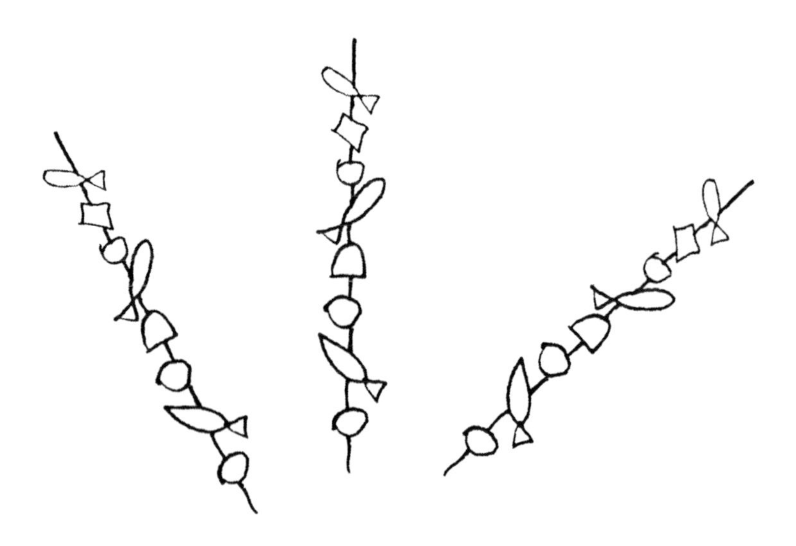

Steamed Mussels or Clams in White Wine Broth

In some areas in Alaska you can get fresh mussels and clams, but it's wonderful that in the freezer section at the local grocery store I found fresh frozen cleaned mussels. Fast, easy, and healthy too.

Ingredients:

1 pound mussels per person (at least), cleaned and beard removed

Broth:

1 cup white wine
1 cup water
1 teaspoon garlic, minced
1 teaspoon dried or fresh parsley, minced
Pinch of fresh-ground pepper, preferably white
1 1-inch piece of lemon zest or lemon grass (optional)
2 juniper berries

Preparation:

In a medium sauce pan add water, white wine, parsley, garlic, pepper, juniper berries, and lemon zest. Put a steamer basket into the same sauce pan, add the mussels, cover.

Bring to a gentle boil for about 8-10 minutes. General precautionary rule – do not eat mussels that do not open up.

Serve mussels with broth on the side in a bowl or put into a large bowl all together. The broth is very tasty.

Serving Suggestion: Serve over linguine.

Suggested Wine:

Chardonnay or Chablis

Shrimp Curry Crepes

A great recipe to serve guests; something special and yet quite easy once you get the hang of it.

Ingredients:

2 12-ounce packages shelled and deveined shrimp
¼ cup butter
½ cup onion, chopped
½ cup celery, diced
¼ cup red pepper, chopped small
1½ cups peeled, cored, and diced cooking apples
4 teaspoons curry powder
¼ cup flour
1 chicken bouillon cube
¼ teaspoon thyme leaves
½ cup heavy cream
½ teaspoon salt

Preparation:

In a 4 quart saucepan over high heat, heat 2 inches of water until boiling. Add shrimp and bring back to boiling for 1 minute until shrimp are tender and pink; drain, cool, and cut into ½-inch pieces.

In a 3-quart saucepan over medium heat, melt butter, add onion and celery; cooking until tender, about 10 minutes. Add apple and curry powder and cook another 5 minutes. Gradually stir in 1 cup water, bouillon, and thyme, stirring until thickened. Use a blender to blend until smooth. Return to saucepan, stir into the sauce, shrimp, cream, and salt. Heat through, spoon ¼ cup mixture onto center of each crepe and roll up.

Crepes from Basic Crepe recipe on the following page.

Basic Crepes

Ingredients:

1 cup flour
1 cup milk
3 eggs, beaten
Pinch salt

Preparation:

Whisk all ingredients together until smooth. Put a tablespoon of butter into a crepe pan over medium heat to coat pan. Pour scant ¼-cup batter into crepe pan. Tip the pan to coat the bottom, and cook for 2 minutes until top is set (underside just brown). Carefully, with a spatula, lift edge of crepe all around, shake pan gently so crepe will come loose. Flip over; cook for 1 minute or until light brown. Slip crepe on a parchment paper-lined cookie sheet, keep warm in the oven, repeat.

Pan Fried Trout 

Make sure to bring along a good heavy-bottomed frying pan when going camping, because there is nothing like fresh Pan Fried Trout.

Ingredients:

trout (dredge in flour)
flour (just enough to coat fish)
3 tablespoons olive oil or vegetable oil
salt and pepper to taste

Preparation:

In a large and heavy frying pan, heat up to medium-high heat; add olive oil, heat 30 seconds. Now add trout to pan and cook for approximately 20 minutes per side.

Alternative:

If you don't happen to have any flour, instant potato flakes work great!

Chapter 3
Wild Alaskan Salmon

Salmon Strudel

Usually when people think of strudel, they think of a sweet strudel, but a savory strudel works great for a delicious entree or brunch.

Ingredients:

1 16-ounce package frozen phyllo (feeloh) dough
½ pound cooked salmon (baked, broiled, steamed, or smoked), flaked into pieces
1 8-ounce package whipped cream cheese
¼ cup sour cream
1 egg, slightly beaten
Zest of 1 lemon
2 teaspoons lemon juice
1 teaspoon lemon pepper
½ cup melted butter

Preparation:

Preheat oven to 350° F.

Mix together the cream cheese, sour cream, lemon zest, lemon juice, lemon pepper, and beaten egg.

Butter a 9 x 12-inch baking dish, start layering the phyllo dough, and brush each sheet with the melted butter. After 6 sheets, spread with the cream cheese mixture, then sprinkle the salmon evenly all around. Layer with 6 more sheets of phyllo, brushing each with the melted butter.

Bake for 1 hour or until a golden brown.

Let cool for 5 minutes. Serve warm or at room temperature.

Suggested Wine:

Champagne or Gewürztraminer (off dry)

Alaskan-Style Blackened Salmon or Shrimp

We eat this camping a lot. Fish right from the stream into the pan!

Ingredients:

2 pounds salmon fillets, pat dry with a paper towel

Seasoning Mixture: (make your own or use my favorite)

1 teaspoon ground white pepper
¼ teaspoon cayenne pepper, ground
1 teaspoon fresh ground black pepper
⅛ teaspoon granulated garlic

Preparation:

Blend all the seasoning together well. Sprinkle generously over the salmon. On high heat, place a large cast iron pan. Heat pan until it is smoking hot—you might need to open the windows, doors, turn on the vent. Do not leave it unattended!

Place the salmon in the pan, cooking until each side is blackened, approximately 8-10 minutes per side.

For shrimp, use completely peeled large shrimp. You should only have to cook them 3–4 minutes per side to blacken.

Note, some people use oil on the pan. I do not recommend it!

Suggested Wine:

Petit Sirah or Chablis

Gravlax (grahv-lahks)

So many Alaskans make good smoked salmon. I once went to a Potlatch, in honor of Violet Reddington, and there were at least 20 different kinds of smoked salmon. But not Lox! So here is a fantastic recipe for Lox.

Ingredients:

2 4-pound salmon fillets – skin on, bones removed;
use super fresh sockeye (red) or coho (silver) salmon.
½ cup sugar
½ cup kosher salt
Fresh dill (approximately 4 sprigs)
2 lemons cut into thin slices

Preparation:

Pat dry the salmon fillets. Mix together the sugar and salt. In a large Ziploc baggie put a layer of the salt/sugar mixture; then put the salmon, skin side down, on the mixture. Cover the top of the salmon with more of the salt/sugar mixture. Lay the lemon slices on next, then the dill sprigs. Put salt/sugar mixture on the second fillet, on both sides. Place the 2nd fillet on top of the 1st fillet, skin side out. Now it looks like a stuffed fish; zip up the baggie.

Put into the refrigerator and turn over twice a day for 3 days. On the 3rd day, gently rinse the fillets, and then pat dry. Slice thinly on the bias but not through the skin.

Serving Suggestions:

On a toasted bagel, spread cream cheese, then spread slices of lox.

Top with sprinkles of capers or minced purple onions.

Suggested Wine:

Champagne

Coconut-Macadamia Nut Salmon Nuggets

They're so good and rich you only need 3 or 4 pieces per person! Cashews also work well.

Ingredients:

2 pounds thick salmon (remove skin and bones), cut into 2 x 2-inch nuggets
2 cups whole wheat flour
½ teaspoon cayenne pepper
Water – enough to make a sticky thick batter
1 cup macadamia nuts, chopped small, roasted in oven at 275° F for 15 minutes
1 cup coconut, shredded, toast in oven at 275° F for 15 minutes
¼ cup vegetable oil or more (You might have to clean the skillet between batches)

Preparation:

In a bowl mix the flour, salt, and cayenne pepper with enough water to make a sticky thick batter. In a pie pan mix together coconut and macadamia nuts. Dip salmon nuggets into the flour mixture then into the coconut/macadamia nut mixture.

In a heavy skillet, heat the oil on medium-high to high heat. Carefully place the salmon nugget into the oil, browning on all sides. Serving when still quite hot is the best.

Suggested Wine:

Riesling or Gewürztraminer (off dry)

Salmon Nicoise (composed salad)

A famous dish from the French Riviera. Nicoise is a beautiful composed salad served on large platters. This is a great way to serve cooked and cold food at the same time. Your guests will be able to eat what, when, and how much they want. Traditionally, tuna is used, but here in Alaska, I use salmon, of course. Serves 4-6.

Ingredients:

2 pounds salmon fillets, Herb-Crusted baked*
8 red potatoes, boiled until just done and sliced into large chunks
Onions, oven roasted†
Green beans, blanched in boiling water for 4 minutes; sliced diagonally about 3–4 inches long
4- to 6 large tomatoes, cut into wedges
4 eggs, hard boiled, cut into quarters
1 cup black or nicoise olives
1 small jar marinated artichoke hearts
4 garlic heads, Roasted‡
Blueberry Vinaigrette Dressing**
Anchovies (optional)
Marinated mushrooms

Preparation:

On a very large platter, arrange in groups: the potatoes, salmon, onions, green beans, tomatoes, olives, eggs, artichokes, roasted garlic and marinated mushrooms. Lay the anchovies here and there, if used. Drizzle the Blueberry Vinaigrette Dressing all over the whole platter; serve buffet style.

Herb-Crusted Salmon:

Preheat oven to 350° F.

Pat the fillets dry; put them on a greased cooking sheet.

Blend together the following:

2 tablespoons minced parsley
1 tablespoon minced garlic
2 tablespoons olive oil
1 teaspoon capers, smashed
2 teaspoons lemon juice

Preheat oven to 350° F.

Cover the salmon with this mixture, cook for 25 minutes. Cool.

†Onions:

Quarter the onions, drizzle with a little olive oil and a pinch of salt. Place on baking sheet and roast for approximately 20 minutes. Cool.

‡Garlic:

Slice whole head in half (horizontally), drizzle with olive oil, and sprinkle with salt. Place on a baking sheet. Bake for 20 minutes or until tender. Place on platter just like they are. Each guest can have a whole half head of garlic.

**Blueberry Vinaigrette Dressing:

¼ cup champagne vinegar or rice vinegar
½ cup olive oil
2 teaspoons Dijon mustard
1 teaspoon shallots, minced
3 tablespoons blueberry jam
1 teaspoon sugar

Put all the ingredients into a bowl except the olive oil. Whisk all the ingredients together, then slowly stream in the olive oil; this will help with the emulsion (blending process).

Suggested Wine:

Champagne or Sancerre

Salmon Taquitos

A refreshing twist on beef taquitos, healthier but every bit as good as the traditional recipe.

Ingredients:

1½ pounds fresh Alaskan salmon
2 packages (12 ea) corn tortillas
Vegetable oil

Preparation:

Pat salmon dry with paper towels. Cut into 4-inch lengths about 1-inch wide, set aside.

Heat about 3 tortillas in the microwave for about 8–10 seconds, or heat in a frying pan until warm and pliable.

In a large frying pan, add enough oil to cover about ¼ inch up the pan, turn on medium heat.

Roll up the salmon strip in a corn tortilla, hold the edge closed with tongs, and lower them gently into oil. Hold with tongs until they are cooked enough to not come undone, then continue cooking until they are browned and crispy. Carefully remove and place on a paper towel. Repeat the process until you are done.

Serving Suggestion: serve with Green Chili Sauce, guacamole, or salsa.

Suggested Wine:

Pinot Blanc

Salmon Potstickers

A healthy and extremely tasty alternative to the traditional recipe that is usually made with ground pork.

Ingredients:

⅓ pound salmon, cooked and flaked (your choice of cooking methods)
½ cup cabbage, shredded and chopped
⅛ cup green onions, finely chopped
1 tablespoon soy sauce
½ tablespoon dry white wine
½ can water chestnuts
½ tablespoon salt
½ teaspoon cornstarch
Dash of pepper
Gyoza wraps*
⅓ cup chicken stock
2 tablespoons vegetable or peanut oil
⅛ cup soy sauce, 3 teaspoons vinegar, and 1 teaspoon chili oil,* mixed together, for condiment

Preparation:

Mix ingredients for filling in bowl. Place a teaspoon of mixture in center of Gyoza skin. Moisten sides with water and fold in half. Gently press sides together to stick and press any air out.

Heat 2 tablespoons oil in frying pan. Add gyoza, side by side upright in pan. Cook over medium heat until bottoms are golden brown. Pour in chicken stock and immediately cover pan tightly. Lower flame and cook until all stock is absorbed, approximately 3 minutes. Serve while hot with soy sauce, vinegar, and chili oil on the side.

*found in your local grocery store.

Suggested Wine:

Riesling or Sémillon

Salmon Egg Rolls

I love developing new and wonderful recipes for salmon that get my salmon-jaded Alaskan friends to delight in salmon once again!

Ingredients:

2 cups cooked flaked salmon (baked, grilled or steamed – carefully remove all of the bones and skin)
1 small onion, diced small
1 large potato, diced small
3 stalks celery, diced medium
1 small head of cabbage, chopped small but not too small
2 teaspoons minced garlic
Pinch of salt
½ teaspoon of pepper
1 package egg roll wrappers
2 tablespoons vegetable oil, enough to fry the egg rolls in

Preparation:

Makes about 20 eggrolls.

In a large deep fry pan, heat pan with the oil. Add potatoes and cook until tender, add celery and cook for 2 minutes. Add garlic, salt and pepper. Then add the cabbage and cook until wilted. Add in the salmon, stir and remove from stove. Set aside and let cool.

Open egg roll wrapper package and set the stack on an angle with a point directed towards you. Put two heaping tablespoons of filling in the middle and then take the point closest to you and fold over the filling. Then fold each side in about 2 inches, then roll up tight, but not too tight or they will break when cooked. Use a finger dipped in water to seal the edge.

In a large frying pan, pour enough oil in to cover about ¼ inch up the pan. Turn the heat up to about medium-high. Put the egg rolls carefully into the pan and fry, turning them until all sides are golden brown. Remove to paper towels to drain.

Serving Suggestion:

Serve with your choice of a dipping sauce; all available in the Asian section of your local grocery store.

Sweet and Sour Sauce
Sweet Chili Sauce
Soy Sauce
Hot Mustard

Suggested Wine:

Rosé (dry) or Pinot Gris

Salmon Cakes

We always like the salmon we prepare for dinner, but my daughter Desiree and I love to use the leftover salmon to make salmon cakes. It has been a much-loved appetizer fare at my caterings for a long time. Use leftover salmon that has been baked, steamed, grilled, or poached. We make 3-inch patties; small and cute and perfect for appetizers.

Ingredients:

1½ pounds cooked salmon (de-boned)
¾ cup onion, minced (you can use sautéed shallots, leeks, or green onions)
½ cup bread crumbs (alternatives – cracker crumbs, or fine oatmeal)
1 teaspoon Worcestershire sauce
½ teaspoon lemon juice
½ teaspoon fresh ground white pepper
1 egg, slightly beaten
1 teaspoon parsley, minced—fresh or dried

Preparation:

Mix all ingredients together. Form into a patty, large or small. In a frying pan, put a small amount of extra virgin olive oil, medium heat. Put patties into pan and brown well on both sides.

Other alternative ingredients:

Minced black or green olives
Minced celery

Serving Suggestion:

Goes great with the Remoulade Sauce on p. 41.

Suggested Wine:

Chenin Blanc or a Rosé (semi-dry)

Chapter 4
Ocean Fresh Halibut

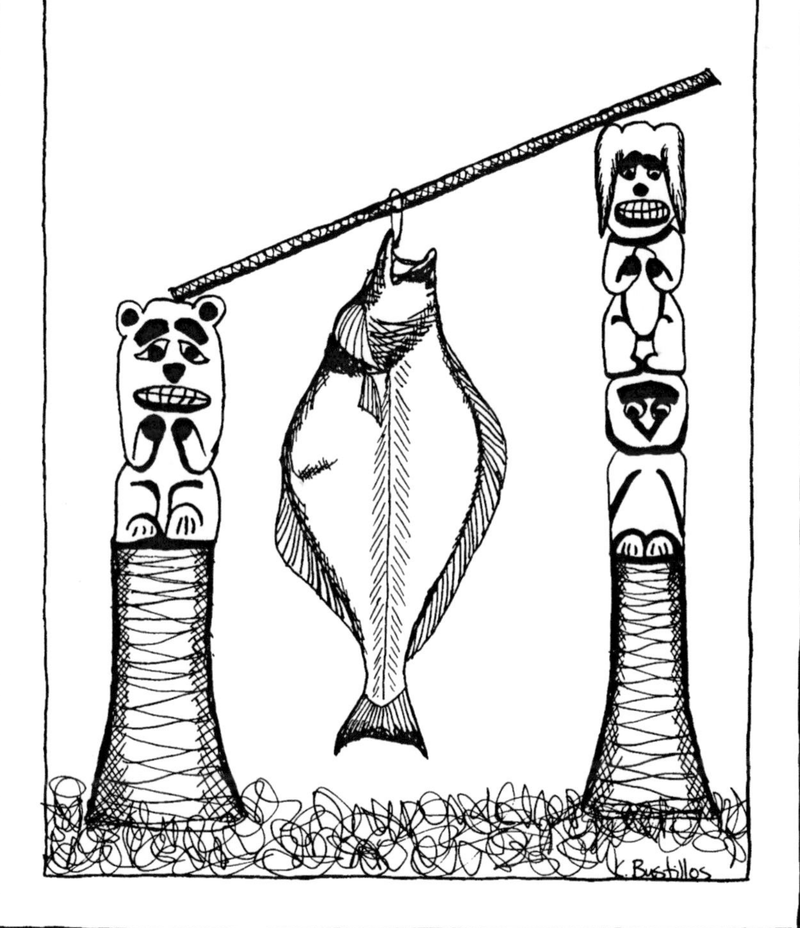

Beer Battered Halibut

Halibut, ling cod, burbot, and even shark work well for frying in this batter. Alaskan Amber Beer® is what I use; it adds a nice smoky richness to the batter. Cornstarch is the secret to an extra-crispy crust.

Ingredients:

1½ pounds fish, deboned and cut into 3-inch chunks
1½- to 2 cups flour
1 large egg (beaten)
¾ cup Alaskan Amber Beer®
½ teaspoon salt
½ teaspoon pepper
¼ cup cornstarch
1 teaspoon Spike (found in your natural food section)
Vegetable oil (for frying)

Preparation:

Mix all the ingredients together except for the fish. Dip the fish into the batter, then deep fry at 350° F. for 3- to 4 minutes or until golden brown. Drain on paper towels.

Oven Baked Fries (chips)

Ingredients:

3 large potatoes
2 tablespoons olive oil
1 teaspoon Spike

Preparation:

Preheat oven to 350° F.

Cut potatoes into large wedges, toss in a large bowl with olive oil and Spike. Bake in the oven about 45 minutes or until crispy brown

Suggested Wine:

Riesling or Chablis

Remoulade Sauce (ray-muh-lahd)

A very sophisticated tartar sauce if you have picky eaters. Blend sauce until smooth, serve on top or alongside, and they will never know why it's so flavorful. I like mine with a little texture.

Ingredients:

½ cup mayonnaise
2 tablespoons Dijon mustard
2 green onions (scallions) sliced thin, both the white and green parts
2 anchovy filets, finely chopped
2 small gherkins, minced small
1 teaspoon parsley
Pinch of salt
2 pinches white or black pepper
2 teaspoons capers, minced
Little squeeze of fresh lemon

Preparation:

Mix all together. Serve chilled or at room temperature.

Tastes great on salmon (steamed, poached, baked, grilled or fried).

Spicy Remoulade: same as above except add 2 tablespoons Louisiana hot sauce.

Halibut Timbales (Tim-bah-lees)

These molded halibut timbales are stuffed with a razor clam stuffing and served with a Remoulade sauce, a very clever presentation so delicious and easy to make. You can substitute crab for the razor clams. I use crab bouillon in the stuffing, but I know it is hard to find; you can use vegetable stock or fish stock instead.

Ingredients:

You will need:

1 muffin pan (large size)
Italian leaf parsley
extra virgin olive oil
2- to 3 pounds of halibut

For the Stuffing:

1 package cubed seasoned croutons or seasoned bread crumbs
3 stalks celery, minced small
1 small onion, minced small
1 medium carrot, minced into tiny cubes
1 pound razor clams or crab, diced
3 tablespoons parsley leaf, minced
1 egg white
¾ cup crab stock or vegetable or seafood stock
2 tablespoons dry sherry
extra virgin olive oil

Preparation:

Preheat oven to 350°F.

In a medium sauté pan on medium heat, put a little olive oil. Sauté onions until they are translucent. Add celery and carrots, cook for approximately 2 minutes. Add stock, sherry, and parsley and cook another 2 minutes. Add clams, cook another 2 minutes. Add bread crumbs or croutons and egg white. Toss it all together and set aside to cool.

Oil the large muffin pans well. Pick a beautiful parsley leaf and lay it in the bottom of each cup. Then put a piece of halibut on the bottom of each muffin cup (¼- to ½-inch thick). Put a piece on each side also. Fill the middle with the stuffing mix. Cover with another piece of halibut.

Fill a large, deep roasting pan with 1 inch of water. Put the muffin pan on top of the roasting pan, cover with foil. Bake for 20 minutes at 350°F. Remove from the oven and let it rest for 5 minutes. They will pop out of the muffin pan easily. Serve with Remoulade sauce (p. 41). You can add your choice of herbs to the sauce, like tarragon or dill. You get the idea!

Suggested Wine:

Chardonnay (buttery)

Halibut with Chanterelles and Caramelized Onions

Chanterelles are a delicate-tasting mushroom, just perfect with halibut, although you can use any of your favorite mushrooms except portobellos in this recipe.

Ingredients:

2 1-pound pieces of halibut, thick cut
Approximately 4 ounces fresh chanterelles or dried, reconstituted in warm water
1 large onion, sliced
4 tablespoons butter
Salt and pepper
3 strips bacon, cooked and chopped small

Preheat oven to 350° F.

Preparation:

In a medium frying pan over medium-high heat, place butter and onions. Cooking until caramelized—a rich brown color. Add in mushrooms and toss, cooking for another 3–5 minutes. Add cooked bacon. Remove from heat to cool.

Make a pocket in each piece of fish; stuff each piece of halibut with half the mushroom/onion mixture. Place into a buttered 8 x 13 x 2-inch glass baking pan. Salt and pepper the fish. Cover with foil and bake for 25 minutes.

Suggested Wine:

Chardonnay or Sauvignon Blanc

Halibut Provençal

My Alaskan take on a dish from a region in Southeastern France. Fresh halibut, hothouse tomatoes, and onions. Serves 3-4.

Ingredients:

2 pounds halibut
6- to 8 large tomatoes (hothouse or fresh is best)
3 cloves garlic (smashed and minced)
4 tablespoons olive oil (a good extra virgin is best)
1 small onion, diced
⅓ cup kalamata olives, pitted

Preheat oven to 350° F.

Preparation:

Mix together tomatoes, onions, garlic, and olives. Pour into a baking dish or cast iron frying pan, place the fish on top. Drizzle olive oil all over the fish. Bake for 25-30 minutes. Serve with rice or roasted potatoes.

Optional alternatives you could add:

Mushrooms
Anchovies
Egg plant
½ teaspoon chili flakes
Bell peppers
Olives

Suggested Wine:

Chardonnay or Sancerre

Halibut Tacos with Blueberry Salsa

The blueberries complement the halibut so well, it will make the flavors pop.

Ingredients:

1 pound halibut, cooked (fried, grilled or baked)
12 corn tortillas

Preparation:

Heat tortillas in a dry frying pan or fry them in oil until soft or crunchy, depending on how you like them. Put about 2- to 3 tablespoons cooked, warm halibut into your warm tortillas. Add 1 or 2 tablespoons blueberry salsa.

Blueberry Salsa

Ingredients:

½ cup tomato, diced
½ cup blueberries
1 small onion, diced
1 jalapeno, minced fine
¼ cup cilantro (optional)
Dash of salt
3 teaspoons of Tapatio hot sauce*
1 teaspoon lemon juice

Preparation:

Mix all together and chill for at least an hour to allow flavors to blend.

Suggested Wine:

Sauvignon Blanc

---

*available in most grocery stores

Halibut Oriental

One of the most conveniently perfect ways to prepare fish: self-steaming little packages of infused flavor goodness. This works well with different seafood and seasonings. Experiment!

Ingredients:

1½ pounds halibut
6 green onions, sliced diagonally and thin, both green and white parts
1 stalk lemon grass, white part sliced thin
Parchment paper* cut into 8 x 8-inch squares

Preparation:

Mix all the following ingredients together:

⅛ cup soy sauce
⅛ cup sherry
2 teaspoons ginger, grated
2 tablespoons garlic, smashed and chopped
Pinch white or lemon pepper

Cut halibut into individual pieces, approximately 3 x 3 inches, 1½ inches thick.

Set each piece of fish onto the piece of parchment paper. Top with a little green onion and lemon grass. Spoon 1½ teaspoons of sauce onto the fish. Fold up the parchment paper into little packages and turn over. Put the packets on a baking sheet and bake for 20 minutes at 350°F.

Suggested Wine:

Chablis

---

*available in grocery stores

Halibut and Crab Enchiladas

This is a favorite dish of my husband, John. Serve with black beans, Spanish rice and a salad. Crab is the dominate flavor, adding halibut stretches out the richness of the crab. The black beans and Spanish rice recipes are in my first cookbook, Suzette's International Cooking.

Ingredients:

1 pound halibut (bake at 350° F. for 25 minutes or until done)
½ pound crab, cooked
2 tablespoons shallots or onions, minced
2 teaspoons lemon juice
12 corn tortillas
2 19-ounce cans green chili verde enchilada sauce
4 ounces queso fresco cheese* or mozzarella would work

Preheat oven to 350° F.

Preparation:

Flake cooked halibut into a bowl, also flake the crab meat into the same bowl. Add shallots, lemon juice and ¼ cup chili verde sauce; stir gently. In a jellyroll or baking pan (8 x 11½ x 2 inches), pour the chili verde sauce, covering about ½ inch deep. Place tortillas into a dry frying pan on medium high heat, cooking until just soft. Remove tortillas from the pan, add 3 tablespoons seafood mixture, roll them and place seam side down into the chili verde sauce. When they are all stuffed, cover with the rest of the chili verde sauce (until they are covered, not swimming), sprinkle with the cheese. Bake for 30 minutes or until gently bubbling.

Suggested Wine:

Sémillon or Malbec

---

*available in most grocery stores in the specialty cheese section

Chapter 5
Simple Suppers and Super Sides

Smoked Salmon and Dill Savory Cheesecake

Looks just like a cheesecake, but you eat it on crackers or French bread. A real stunner.

Crust:

1 cup cracker crumbs (Ritz or saltines, any will work, turned into crumbs)
½ cup butter, melted

Preparation:

Mix together in a bowl, then press into a pie pan. Set aside for now.

Filling:

3 8-ounce packages cream cheese, room temperature
2 cups sour cream
3 eggs, lightly beaten
1 cup smoked salmon, flaked
1 teaspoon dried dill weed
½ teaspoon salt
Zest of 1 lemon
½ teaspoon lemon pepper

Preparation:

Preheat oven to 350° F.

Whip all ingredients together until very smooth. Pour into the crumb-filled pie pan. Bake for 60 minutes or until it doesn't jiggle in the middle. Let cool completely. Serve with crackers.

Suggested Wine:

Prosecco (Italy)

Stuffed Zucchini

Here in Alaska the average size of a zucchini at the local farmers market is about 15 inches long and 8 inches around. Perfect for stuffing!

Ingredients:

1 large zucchini (at least 12 inches long). Wash and slice in half lengthwise, and scoop out the pulp
½ pound ground veal or moose
4 tablespoons cooked chorizo (chor-ee-zoh) minced
½ small onion, minced
2 cloves garlic, smashed and minced
1 teaspoon parsley, minced
¼ teaspoon salt
¼ teaspoon pepper
¼ cup salsa
½ cup potato chips, crumbled
⅛ cup bread crumbs
½ cup grated parmesan cheese
1 tablespoon vegetable oil

Preparation:

Preheat oven to 350° F.

Mix meat, chorizo, onion, garlic, parsley, salt, pepper, bread crumbs, and salsa in a bowl. Pat into zucchini halves, top with crumbled potato chips. Bake on a cookie sheet for 1 hour. Remove from the oven, sprinkle with cheese and bake for 5 more minutes.

Suggested Wine:

Chenin blanc or White Zinfandel

Stuffed Mushrooms

These have always brought on the ooohs and aahhhs. . . .

Ingredients:

24 large mushrooms, 1½- to 2 inches in diameter. Wipe off with paper towel if necessary and remove stems

Preparation:

On a cookie sheet, place mushrooms stem side up. Cook until a pool of liquid forms in the middle, approximately 8–12 minutes. Keep an eye on them. When they are done, remove from the oven, and paper towel off the water beads. Set aside. Mince up the stems and set aside.

Ingredients:

1 8-ounce package cream cheese, room temperature
8 ounces bulk caribou or pork sausage
¼ teaspoon or pinch cayenne pepper
2 tablespoons shallots or onion, minced
¼ cup bread crumbs
1 teaspoon dried parsley

Preheat oven to 350° F.

Preparation:

Fry the sausage and cayenne until done. Put into a medium bowl to cool. Add mushroom stems, cream cheese, and shallots to cooled sausage mixture.

Form into small balls and set on top of each mushroom. Dust with bread crumbs. Put a pinch of parsley on top in the middle. Bake for 15 to 20 minutes, until heated throughout.

Suggested Wine:

Chardonnay

49th State Carbonara (Kar-boh-nah-rah)

I used to cater for the Yountville Market in Yountville, California. With the whole deli at my disposal I had a great time. This is a very, very special recipe. Fresh peas are a prolific crop in the Matanuska Valley and make a great addition to this recipe; you'll love it.

Ingredients:

1 pound spaghetti noodles, cooked al dente* (set aside)
4 thin slices panchetta,† cut into small pieces, using scissors
1 large ripe tomato, diced (preferably hothouse or homegrown)
2 cups half and half
1 cup parmesan cheese, grated
¼ cup butter (real)
½ cup fresh peas, shelled

Preparation:

In a large frying pan, fry the panchetta until lightly brown, add tomato and cook 1 minute. Add butter, but do not let it brown. As soon as butter is melted, add the half and half, stir; add peas, stir; sprinkle with cheese a little at a time, stirring gently. It should be thick but not too thick. Add cooked noodles, toss well and serve.

Optional: grate a clove of fresh garlic over the top, just before serving.

Suggested Wine:

Sauvignon Blanc

---

*al dente – just slightly undercooked
†panchetta – non-smoked bacon, ask at your local deli

Yellow Squash Casserole Deluxe

Ingredients:

1½ teaspoons extra virgin olive oil
4 medium yellow squash, cut into ¼-inch slices
¼ pound chantrelle mushrooms, very coarsly chopped (substitute with oyster, morel, crimini or button mushrooms if needed)
6- to 8-ounce jar (or can) artichoke hearts (not pickled), drained and sliced into quarters
6 tablespoons onion, minced
½ cup bread crumbs
¼ cup parmesan cheese

Preparation:

Preheat oven to 350° F.

Toss squash and mushrooms into a bowl with the olive oil; add onions and artichokes. Place into a 9 x 12 x 2-inch baking dish. Mix bread crumbs and parmesan cheese together; spread over the top of the casserole. Bake for 40 minutes or until golden brown.

Suggested Wine:

Semillon

Matanuska Roasted Root Vegetables

Once again my trip to the U-Pick farm in the Matanuska Valley yielded a lot of wonderful, fresh fall vegetables to create fantastic dishes with. White turnips, white beets with pink tops, fingerling potatoes, sweet carrots, parsnips, rutabagas, and onions. You can also do a summer vegetable version. Rule of thumb: use what you like.

Ingredients:

½ teaspoon Spike*
3 tablespoons extra virgin olive oil
2 pounds of a variety of root veggies

Preparation:

Wash (peel when necessary) and cut the veggies into 1½-inch cubes. Pat dry with paper towels. Toss in with the olive oil and Spike. Put into a roasting pan. Bake for approximately 40 minutes at 350°F. Keep an eye on them; when they are golden brown and tender they are done.

Serving Suggestion: the leftovers are so versatile you can use them in a soup, a frittata (crustless quiche), or chopped up in a pasta salad. Have fun with them, use your imagination.

Suggested Wine:

Pinot blanc

---

*Spike is a wonderful blend of spices. I use it a lot. It can be found in the health food section of the store. Sometimes you can purchase it in bulk.

Artichoke Fritters–Light, Fluffy, and Crispy

On a recent visit to a U-Pick farm in the Matanuska Valley, to my delight I discovered they grow artichokes. Having found the fabulously large globes growing here inspired me to create this recipe.

Ingredients:

1½ cups cooked artichoke meat, chopped into pea-size pieces*
2 egg whites

Mix the following ingredients together.

¾ cup flour
1 teaspoon sugar
⅓ teaspoon salt
1½ teaspoons baking powder
¼ teaspoon Spike†

Preparation:

Beat the 2 egg whites until fluffy but not stiff.

Toss the artichoke bits in the egg whites, then into the flour until just incorporated.

Heat ½ inch of vegetable oil in a medium frying pan, on medium-high heat. Drop the artichoke mixture by tablespoonful into oil. Pat down just a little. Wait to try to turn them over. When they are golden brown they will lift right up. Turn them over and cook until dark golden brown. Serve immediately.

I keep a little spray bottle with water and a few tablespoons lemon juice handy so I can spray a little on things that tend to darken rapidly like artichokes.

Suggested dip: garlic aioli (mayo)

Suggested Wine:

Rosé or Viognier

*I scraped the tender meat from each leaf with a teaspoon, but you can also use just the heart meat.

†Spike is a wonderful blend of spices. I use it a lot. It can be found in the health food section of the store. Sometimes you can purchase it in bulk.

Corn Fritters

The Alaska State Fair has a wonderful corn fritter booth, which I can't resist. Here is my version of their fritters.

Ingredients:

1 can whole kernel corn, drained
1 large ear of corn; coarsely grate corn off the cob, drain
1 egg yolk
1 egg white
4 tablespoons sugar
¼ teaspoon salt
½ cup flour
⅛ cup buttermilk

Preparation:

Mix all ingredients together except egg white. In a separate bowl, whip the egg white until fluffy but not dry. Fold the egg white into the rest of the mixture. Batter should hold together well; if not, add a little more flour until you have a nice and thick batter.

In a heavy pot or Dutch oven, add enough vegetable oil to approximately 5 inches deep. Heat to approximately 375° F. Using a medium-size ice cream scoop, carefully drop batter into the oil. Fry the fritters until they are golden brown, turning them over to cook evenly.

Serve with Honey Butter – ½ cup butter at room temperature, mixed with 4 tablespoons honey

Suggested Wine:

Liebfraumilch or Chablis

Baked Tomatoes

A very nice accompaniment to so many meals, like BBQ, roast, etc. When you break into the tomato, the juice integrates and mingles with the other flavors on the plate, bringing it all together. Use just slightly underripe tomatoes. Serves 4–8.

Ingredients:

4 large slightly underripe tomatoes
8 tablespoons bread crumbs
4 tablespoons grated parmesan cheese
½ teaspoon dried parsley

Preheat oven to 350° F.

Preparation:

Mix together bread crumbs, cheese, and parsley. Slice tomatoes in the middle, horizontally. Top each tomato with 1½ tablespoons crumb mixture. Cover small baking sheet with parchment paper or non-stick spray, then carefully place the tomatoes.

Bake for 45–60 minutes or until golden brown on top.

Suggested Wine:

Pinot Grigio or Chenin Blanc

Tundra Tandoori Chicken 

One time we were on a camping trip, and we forgot to bring a grate for the fire pit. I had a plastic container full of Tandoori chicken, so I looked around and found a large flat stone. We made coals in the fire, set the rocks right onto the coals and then cooked the chicken sizzling away right there on those rocks. It turned out really good too.

Ingredients:

1 package bamboo skewers, soaked in water*
1 medium onion, diced
1 clove garlic
3 tablespoons vegetable oil
2 tablespoons lemon juice
1 teaspoon salt
1½ teaspoons ground coriander
1 teaspoon sugar
½ teaspoon ground cumin
½ teaspoon turmeric
¼ teaspoon ground cardamon
¼ teaspoon cayenne pepper
¼ cup plain yogurt
3 pounds chicken breasts (skinned and boned), cut into 3- to 4-inch chunks

Preparation:

In a blender container, place all the ingredients except chicken and yogurt. Cover and blend on high speed until mixture is all pureed. Pour into a 12 x 8-inch baking dish, stir in the yogurt. Add chicken to the yogurt mixture, cover and refrigerate at least 12 hours, turning occasionally. Put the meat onto the skewers, leaving about 3 inches on each end. About 1¼ hours before serving, prepare the grill for cooking. When the grill is ready, place the chicken over low coals, cook about 35 minutes or until chicken is fork tender, turning frequently and basting with some of the yogurt mixture.

The marinated meat can be made ahead and frozen for up to a week before then placing on skewers.

Suggested Wine:

Sangiovese or Syrah

---

*available in most markets

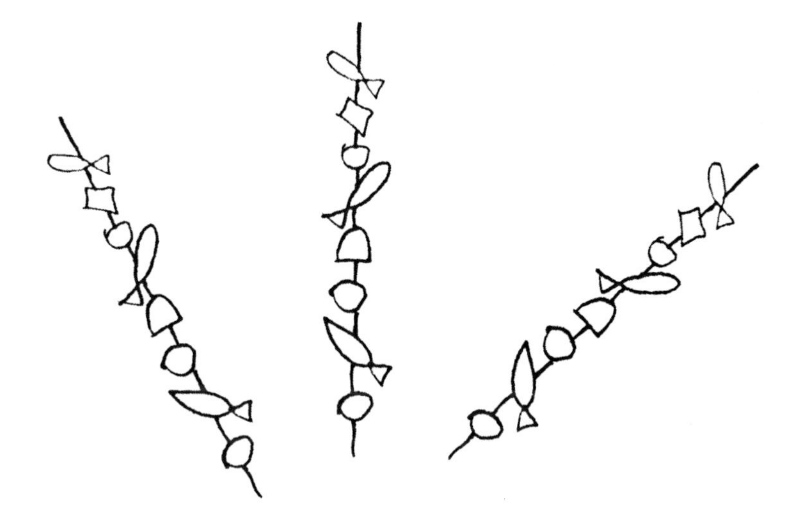

Pozole (Pork or Goat) 

If you like hominy, you'll love this classice Mexican soup. Tender pork or goat and just the right amount of heat, makes this hearty dish just perfect on a cold winter day.

Ingredients:

1 pound pork tenderloin or boneless pork chops, cut into bite-size cubes
2 cans white hominy, drained
2 tablespoons vegetable oil
8 cloves garlic, smashed and chopped
1 medium onion, chopped
2 quarts chicken broth
6 teaspoons green chilis, chopped
½ jalepeno pepper, minced
¼ teaspoon black pepper
⅛ teaspoon cayenne
½ teaspoon chili powder
1 teaspoon oregano leaves, crushed
½ teaspoon ground cumin
¼ bunch cilantro leaves (no stems), roughly chopped

Preparation:

In a large 3- or 4-quart stockpot or Dutch oven, place vegetable oil; turn heat to medium high. Add the pork bites and fry until well browned. Add garlic for 20 seconds; do not allow to brown (it will turn bitter). Add onion and cook for 1 minute. Add the chicken broth and continue to cook for 20 minutes on medium low until the meat is tender. Now add the rest of the ingredients, except for the cilantro; that goes in at the last minute to give it some freshness.

Suggested Wine:

Merlot or Petit Syrah

Chapter 6
One Pot Meals

Alaskan Goulash

I once worked in a Hungarian restaurant in Reno, Nevada. The food was so good! I especially loved the goulash. It works so well using moose.

Ingredients:

2 pounds moose meat or beef (sirloin works well), cut into 1½- to 2-inch cubes
3 large potatoes, cubed
1 large onion, diced
2 bell peppers, diced (I use red, but use what you like)
3 cloves garlic, minced
3 tablespoons paprika
6 large tomatoes, pureed
½ teaspoon red pepper flakes
3 tablespoons flour
3 tablespoons vegetable oil
1 tablespoon beef bouillon

Preparation:

In a medium-size heavy pot, on medium heat, add the vegetable oil. Slowly add the meat, browning on all sides. Stir in the flour. Add the rest of the ingredients. If you find you need a little more liquid, add a little water. Simmer for 1 hour.

Serving suggestion:

Serve in large bowls with a warm, crusty loaf of bread.

Suggested Wine:

Green Hungarian or Gewürztraminer (dry)

Pepper Pot Stew

A Dutch oven (heavy pot) filled with Pepper Pot Stew on a camping trip always hits the right spot. A great recipe for utilizing wild game meat.

Ingredients:

1½ pounds moose stew meat, or beef, cut into 2- or 3-inch cubes
2 cups bell peppers (red, yellow, orange or green—or mix them up), cut into 2- or 3-inch pieces
1 large onion, coarsely chopped
3 tablespoons flour
2 tablespoons Worcestershire sauce
3 cups beef broth
2 large tomatoes, chopped
2 large carrots, sliced 1/8 inch or so
2 tablespoons soy sauce
2 teaspoons dried parsley
2 tablespoons vegetable oil
Salt and Pepper

Preparation:

In a medium stockpot or Dutch oven, fry the meat in vegetable oil until nicely browned; add onions and cook 2 minutes more. Sprinkle with flour; add in beef broth, Worcestershire sauce, salt, and pepper.

Cook on medium heat for 10 minutes. Now add the tomatoes, carrots, soy sauce and parsley. Reduce heat to simmer for 20 more minutes. Serve with rice, potatoes, or polenta.

Suggested Wine:

Pinot Noir or Malbec

Real Chili, Chili Beans

Alaska meets the Southwest in a pot!

Ingredients:

1½ pounds ground moose or lean ground beef
1 large onion, chopped medium
5 Ancho chili peppers* (soak in hot water for 20 minutes)
1 quart or more chicken stock
2 cans kidney beans
2 tablespoons vegetable oil
1 teaspoon sugar
Salt and pepper to taste
½ teaspoon chili flakes

Preparation:

Remove stem and seeds from Ancho chilis that have been soaking. Coarsely chop them up, put them in the blender with ¼- to ½ cup of chicken stock; blend until smooth.

In a large 4-quart stock pot (or very large pot) over medium-high heat, fry the ground meat in the vegetable oil. When it's almost done, add the onion and cook 5 more minutes.

Add the chili mixture, the rest of the chicken stock, and the sugar. Turn the heat down to simmer and cook for 20 minutes. Add the beans and cook for another 20 minutes. If the mixture is too thick, add a little water or more chicken stock. Salt and pepper to taste.

Suggested Wine:

Meritage or Burgundy

---

*available in some grocery stores or specialty markets

Vegetable Garden Soup

This is one of the healthiest soups you can make. A visit to a local farmers market is a great idea.

Ingredients:

10 ripe tomatoes, pureed
1 large potato, peeled, chopped in small squares
4 stalks celery, washed and sliced ¼-inch thick
1 medium onion, diced
1½ quarts vegetable stock
3 large carrots, diced
3 tablespoons olive oil
3- to 4 zucchini, cut into olive-size pieces
10 small mushrooms, quartered
½ head cauliflower, cut into small chunks
1 small head cabbage, (bok choy, swiss chard, or turnip greens), cut into small chunks
2 teaspoons dried basil
1 teaspoon Spike*
1 teaspoon soy sauce
1 teaspoon black pepper

Preparation:

In a heavy large sauce pan, sauté the celery, onion, and dried basil for 5 minutes. Then add the tomato puree, vegetable stock, potato, Spike, pepper, and soy sauce. Simmer for 5 more minutes. Add the zucchini, cauliflower, mushrooms and cabbage; simmer for 15 to 20 minutes longer. Add any other vegetables you like.

Optional: Top with parmesan cheese.

Suggested Wine:

White or Red Zinfandel

---

*available at health food section of your grocery store, or health food store

Stuffed Potato Soup

Another great way to use potatoes!

Ingredients:

5 large baked potatoes (bake at 350° F. for 75 minutes)
5 strips bacon, cooked crispy
½ pound cheddar cheese, shredded
4 tablespoons butter
4 tablespoons flour
1½ quarts milk
Salt and Pepper

Preparation:

Peel the skin off the potatoes and chop into chunks. In a large saucepan, melt the butter over medium-high heat, then stir in the flour; continue cooking for 2 minutes, stirring until smooth. Add the milk, stir and cook for another 2 minutes. Add the potatoes; take a potato masher and mash just a little. Bring mixture to a simmer until the soup thickens. Chop up the bacon, add it to the soup. Season with salt and pepper to taste. Add the cheese, mix well. Simmer for approximately 15 minutes more.

Optional: From the jar, add one jalapeno pepper, smashed up.

Suggested Wine:

Chablis or White Zinfandel

Chowder (Salmon, Halibut, Clam, or Corn)

Who doesn't enjoy a warm, comforting bowl of chowder when it's cold out?

Ingredients:

1½ cups cooked of your choice of salmon, halibut, clams, or corn
2 10-ounce cans clams or corn, reserve liquid
1 small onion, diced small
1 large stalk leek, wash well, and thinly sliced
2 large potatoes, diced medium
2 large celery stalks, washed and sliced
3 tablespoons butter
2 tablespoons flour
4 cups milk
1 cup cream
Optional: clam liquid

Preparation:

In a Dutch oven or heavy pot, melt butter and cook onion on medium-high until tender. Add potatoes, cook until half way done, sprinkle in the flour. Mix well. Add milk, cream, clam liquid, celery and leeks.

Simmer on low for 20 minutes. Add salmon, halibut, clams, or corn and cook another 15 minutes.

If you want to thicken the chowder, mix 3 tablespoons flour into ¼ cup milk, blending well. Add it to the chowder, stirring together. Bring to a boil for 1 minute.

Optional: Dice up 3 strips cooked bacon, stir into chowder.

Suggested Wine:

Sauvignon or Chablis

Alaskan-Style Cioppino (chuh-pee-noh)
Mixed Seafood

In Alaska the seafood is so fresh, abundant, and sweet. Make this recipe with your favorite seafood combination.

Ingredients:

2 tablespoons extra virgin olive oil
½ medium onion, minced small
4 cloves garlic, grated or minced well
2 quarts whole tomatoes in sauce, blended well until smooth (homegrown preferably)
3 tablespoons parsley, minced
½ cup dry white wine, or dry sherry
1 teaspoon Tabasco (optional) I only add this when I am in a spicy mood
3 tablespoons fresh lemon juice
2 pounds mussels, cleaned and de-bearded and in shells
2 pounds crab parts, cleaned in shells
2 pounds clams, cleaned and in shells
1 pound shrimp, rinsed in shells
1 pound scallops, sea scallops or bay scallops (although bay tend to get lost)
Add lobster, if you are being extravagant

Preparation:

In a heavy duty 4-quart stew pan or Dutch oven, sauté onions in olive oil until translucent. Add garlic and cook for 1 minute, then add wine, cook 1 minute longer. Add tomatoes, parsley, and lemon juice and simmer on medium heat for 20 minutes. Add all the seafood and cook for 15-20 minutes. Serve in large bowls with fresh French bread to soak up all the sauce. Serves up to 4.

Suggested Wine:

White Zinfandel or a chardonnay

Northern Lights Gazpacho
(gahz-pah-choh)

Normally served chilled, which is wonderful on a warm summer day. You can also serve this hot. Try it both ways and see which you like best. It's so healthy and a great recipe for your summer vegetables.

Ingredients:

3 cups tomato juice
3 tablespoons olive oil or vegetable oil
3 large tomatoes, peeled and seeded
1 cucumber, peeled and seeded
1 small onion, chopped
1 small green pepper, chopped
1 small garlic clove, peeled
3 tablespoons parsley, chopped
1 teaspoon sugar
¾ teaspoon salt
½ teaspoon hot pepper sauce
3 tablespoons fresh parsley, chopped

Preparation:

In a covered blender container at high speed, blend all ingredients, a third at a time, until finely chopped. Pour into a bowl and chill. When chilled, serve and enjoy.

Optional: Dollop of sour cream as a garnish.

Suggested Wine:

Sauvignon Blanc or White Zinfandel

Wild Rabbit or Hare Stew

There are lots of rabbits and hares in Alaska. Here is a delicious recipe making good use of the juniper berries that grow here. You can also use chicken.

Ingredients:

1 hare or rabbit, cut up
4 tablespoons butter
4 tablespoons flour

Steeping liquid:

½ cup vinegar
½ cup water
4 juniper berries (in the spice section of your grocery)
1 bay leaf
½ teaspoon peppercorns
1 small onion, sliced
Salt and pepper
2 teaspoons lemon juice
½ cup dry white wine, optional

Preparation:

Simmer the steeping ingredients together for 5 minutes, let cool. Pour over the meat and reserve some of the liquid. Let mixture soak for 2 days. Remove meat, letting it drip on paper towels for a couple of minutes. Fry meat in butter until browned on all sides; add onion and cook 3 minutes longer. Add in flour, stirring for 2 more minutes. Add half the reserved steeping liquid, cover and cook until tender about 1½ hours. If necessary, replenish liquid with a little dry white wine or water.

Serves 4.

Suggested Wine:

Syrah or Vouvray (France)

Chapter 7
Main Course Meals

Sausage Gravy

I love biscuits and gravy, but don't trust ordering it in a restaurant; you never know what they might have put in it. It's so simple to make, so I make it at home every so often.

Ingredients

1 pound package ground sausage – moose, caribou, or pork work well (I prefer hot)
4 tablespoons flour
4 cups milk (you could substitute cream for ½ cup milk for extra richness)
1 teaspoon beef bouillon
½ teaspoon pepper

Preparation:

In a heavy skillet, cook the sausage. When it's almost done, sprinkle in the flour, stirring well. Add milk, bring to a mild boil, and then stir in bouillon. Serve over Biscuits

Homemade Biscuits

In Alaska, good biscuits are important. We need them to put our jam and jellies on. And, of course, biscuits and gravy–the super comfort food.

Ingredients:

4 cups flour
2 tablespoons baking powder
3 teaspoons sugar
1 teaspoon salt
1 cup butter (2 sticks), cold, cut into pieces
2 cups heavy cream
1 egg, beaten

Preparation:

Preheat oven to 400° F

In a large bowl, whisk together the flour, baking powder, sugar and salt. Using a pastry blender or butter knife, cut in the butter until it looks like coarse crumbs.

Pour in the cream and use a spatula, folding until the dough comes together. The dough will be slightly sticky. Turn dough onto a lightly floured surface, gently pat dough into a round. Do not overwork dough.

Roll out to about 1 inch thick. Use a 2¼-inch round cutter to cut out the biscuits. Place on an ungreased cookie sheet about 2 inches apart. Brush each biscuit with the egg wash. Bake until golden brown, about 20-25 minutes.

Ptarmigan Kabobs

You can use any flavorful fowl for this recipe, but only use the breast meat. Pheasant, Cornish game hen, or even chicken will work.

Ingredients:

Approximately 18 bamboo skewers, cut in half and soaked in water
4 ptarmigan breasts, cut into ½-inch chunks
8 slices bacon, cut into 1-inch pieces
1 basket of pearl onions, peeled

Marinade:

4 tablespoons balsamic vinegar
¼ cup extra virgin olive oil
2 teaspoons shallot, minced
¼ teaspoon salt
½ teaspoon pepper
1 teaspoon Dijon mustard or 1 teaspoon dry mustard powder

Preparation:

Whisk all marinade ingredients together in a glass bowl. Add the Ptarmigan chunks to the marinade mixture. Refrigerate at least 1 hour.

On the skewers, alternate the meat, onions, and bacon, leaving one inch on each end of the bamboo skewer (so you can hold onto it).

Grill on a barbeque or in a grill pan over medium-high heat, turning often for about 15 – 20 minutes.

I bring these kabobs to the table under a dome of glass. When you lift it up, you release the fragrance and aroma at the table in front of your guests—like pheasant under glass, except it's ptarmigan under glass!

Suggested Wine:

Sangiovese (Italy) or Beaujolais (France)

Ham & Cheddar Cheese Stratta

I use a moose or caribou ham, but a traditional ham works just fine.

Ingredients:

1 small round of French bread, slightly stale or leave out overnight
¼ pound ham, cooked, sliced thin (about the size of a poker chip)
1½ cups cheddar cheese, grated
4 tablespoons parmesan cheese, grated
4 eggs
1 cup ricotta cheese
1 cup heavy cream
1¼ cups milk
½ stick butter, room temperture
½ teaspoon Spike
½ teaspoon pepper

Preparation:

Preheat oven to 350° F.

In a large bowl, whip eggs. Add in ricotta cheese, whip. Add in sugar, whip. Add in Spike, pepper, and cream, whip. Add in milk and whip again.

Butter each slice of bread. In an 8 x 11½ x 2-inch baking dish or slightly larger; alternate layers of bread, ham, and cheese until almost to the top. Pour egg mixture all over; let it soak in for at least 10 minutes. Top with parmesan cheese. Loosely cover with foil and bake for 40 minutes. Remove foil and bake for an additional 20 minutes until golden brown.

Suggested Wine:

Gewürztraminer

Sloppy Yukon Joes

In grade school we were lucky enough to have homemade food in our cafeteria. The sloppy joes were especially good. I have tried so many combinations of sloppy joe recipes until I finally figured out the one that tasted like what I remembered. So simple, but the best!

Ingredients:

1 pound ground moose meat or hamburger
1 8-ounce can tomato sauce
1 medium carrot
8 fresh hamburger buns (warm them, do not toast them)

Preparation:

In a medium frying pan, cook the ground meat until just done. Drain if necessary. Add tomato sauce and simmer for 5 minutes. Grate the carrot into mixture in the pan. Stir a little bit. Serve right away on warmed buns.

Suggested Wine:

Merlot or Zinfandel

Alaskan Cassoulet (Ham Hock, White beans and Caribou Stew)

The flavor of this combination will blow your mind. Put it over rice and it's a complete meal. Here in Alaska we can buy caribou sausage, but you can use andoullie or even a kielbasasa. Use what you prefer.

Ingredients and Preparation:

In a Dutch oven (large heavy pot) place:

1 large ham hock and cover with water. Simmer until it starts to fall apart. Then add

2½ cups white beans and simmer for about 1 hour.

Then add the following ingredients:

1 cup onion, chopped (yellow or white)
1 cup celery, chopped
1 cup green bell pepper, chopped
½ teaspoon cayenne
2 cloves garlic, pressed and minced
1 tablespoon dried parsley
½ teaspoon Spike (found in the natural food section)
½ teaspoon fresh ground black pepper
½ teaspoon fresh ground white pepper
2 cubes chicken bouillon, or 2 teaspoons chicken bouillon powder
1 large carrot, cubed small
2 caribou sausages, sliced into ½-inch slices
1 bay leaf

Simmer for another hour until the beans are done and the flavors have all come together.

Suggested Wine:

Sauvignon Blanc or White Zinfandel

Golden Nugget Empanadas

These small meat pies are flaky, savory, and delicious. At home in Alaska, I use moose, caribou, or bear meat but traditionally you use beef.

Ingredients:

3 tablespoons olive oil
1 onion, minced
¼ green bell pepper, finely chopped
1 pound extra-lean ground beef or moose
½ teaspoon ground cumin
¼ teaspoon paprika
Salt and freshly ground black pepper to taste
½ cup water
⅓ cup raisins
1 hard boiled egg, finely chopped
10 green olives, pitted and finely chopped
2 17-ounce packages frozen puff pastry (defrosted)
Flour for dusting
1 egg white

Preheat oven to 375° F.

Preparation:

In a saucepan, sauté onions, green pepper, ground meat, cumin, paprika, salt and pepper in olive oil until lightly browned. Add water and raisins; then simmer covered until meat is cooked through. Remove from heat and let cool, then fold in the chopped boiled egg and olives.

Thaw puff pastry until completely thawed but still cold and roll out on a floured work surface. Cut pastry with a cookie cutter to make 3½-inch circles. While holding one circle at a time in your hand, spoon 1 teaspoon of meat mixture into the middle. Fold pastry in half and secure the circle by pressing the edges together with a fork to make a seal. Repeat with the remaining ingredients.

Place empanadas on a well-buttered baking sheet and brush the tops with egg white. Bake for 20 minutes or until puff pastry is well puffed and golden. Remove from the oven, let cool, then serve.

Suggested Wine:

Rioja (Spain) or Sherry

Moose Roast with Cranberry Glaze

I always marinate my moose roasts for at least 24 hours. This helps to tenderize and infuse flavor into the roast. And remember, you can substitute any moose recipe with beef.

Moose Roast

For the marinade you will need:

½ cup cranberry juice
6 juniper berries
1/8 cup apple cider vinegar
¼ cup olive oil
1/8 teaspoon salt
1 teaspoon pepper

Preparation:

Preheat oven to 450°F.

Put the roast into a large Ziplock baggie with the marinade; keep in refrigerator for 24 hours, turning roast every few hours. Remove roast and dry well. Put into a roasting pan and put into oven, and cook for 20 minutes at 450°F., then turn oven down to 350°F. Start basting every 5 to 10 minutes with cranberry glaze until done. Continue cooking and use a meat thermometer to reach your desired doneness. Let meat rest for 10 minutes before serving.

Cranberry Glaze

In a small sauté pan, mix:

¼ cup sugar
½ cup cranberry juice
½ stick cinnamon
Cook together for 10 minutes on a medium-high heat.

Suggested Wine:

Carbernet, Pinot Noir, or a Merlot

Ultimate Meat Loaf

Almost any ground meat works for this recipe. My favorite is a moose, elk, caribou, or beef mixture. Turkey would taste good also. For me the wilder the better. And remember, any leftovers make good sandwiches.

Ingredients:

2 pounds lean ground meat (moose, caribou, etc.)
1 medium onion, minced
½ medium yellow bell pepper, minced
½ medium red bell pepper, minced
1 large Portobello mushroom, minced (remove stem and discard)
1 tablespoon Worcestershire sauce
1 teaspoon Tabasco sauce
¾ cup Irish oatmeal (or cracker crumbs or bread crumbs)
2 eggs
¾ teaspoon pepper
½ teaspoon salt

Preparation:

Preheat oven to 350°F.

In a large bowl, gather all the above ingredients. Work them together well for at least 3 minutes. Grease or spray a loaf pan. Form a loaf with the mixture and put into the loaf pan. Bake for approximately 1½ hours. Let meat loaf stand for about 5 minutes before serving. Pour off and discard drippings.

Suggested Wine:

Burgundy or Malbec

Clam Pesto Pizza

This is an unusual recipe for a pizza, but it's really good.

Ingredients:

1 pizza dough recipe (p. 87)
1 5-ounce can fancy whole baby clams, diced
1½ cups mozzarella cheese, shredded
Olive oil
¼ cup white sauce (Béchamel, p. 85)
¼ cup pesto, (p. 86)
1 14-ounce can artichoke hearts, drained, cut into bite-size pieces

Preparation:

Brush the pizza dough circles with olive oil; top with white sauce, spreading it all around. Add pesto by spoonfuls all around. Sprinkle half the calms on each pizza; then half the cheese on each one. Bake on a pizza pan at 400°F for 15-20 minutes until it is the doneness that you prefer.

For a crispier crust: for the last 5 minutes of cooking, slide pizza off the pan directly onto the rack.

Suggested Wine:

Merlot or Pinot Noir

Basic White Sauce (Béchamel) with garlic

A great alternative to tomato sauce for pizza.

Ingredients:

3 tablespoons butter
3 tablespoons all purpose flour
Pinch salt
2 pinches pepper
¼ teaspoon paprika
⅔ cup milk or half and half
1 teaspoon garlic, finely minced

Preparation:

In a small saucepan, over medium heat, melt butter, sprinkle in flour, and stir until smooth. Gradually stir in milk, salt, pepper, garlic and paprika, cooking until thickened and smooth. If it's too thick, add just a little more milk.

Pesto

I grow basil here in Alaska every summer so I can make my own pesto and freeze it to last all winter. Some of the leaves are as big as my hand. This recipe calls for a food processor, but I have used a blender, it's not as easy though.

Ingredients:

4 cups fresh basil leaves, washed and patted towel dry
⅓- to ½ cup extra virgin olive oil
2 cloves garlic, peeled
½ cup roasted pine nuts or walnuts
⅓ cup parmesan cheese, grated
Pinch salt
1½ teaspoons lemon juice (preserves the color and adds a zip of flavor)

Preparation:

In a food processor, add the garlic, half the nuts and leaves; stream in some of the olive oil, and pulse a couple of times. Add the rest of the ingredients. Streaming in the olive oil, pulse a couple more times. Put into sterilized jars, leaving ½-inch head space; cover top with a little olive oil to preserve. Keeps in the refrigerator for approximately 2 weeks, or you can freeze it.

Serving Suggestions:

Serve over noodles, hot or cold

Basic Pizza Dough

Pizza dough is not as hard to make as one might think. Knowing how to make pizza dough is super handy, and there are so many things you can do with it.

Ingredients:

4 cups all purpose flour
1 package active dry yeast
1 teaspoon salt
1½ cups water

Preparation:

In a large bowl, combine yeast, 2 cups flour and salt. In a medium saucepan over low heat, bring water to 120°–130° F. Mix water into dry ingredients, and add the rest of the flour a ¼ cup at a time.

On a floured surface, knead dough about 6 minutes. Roll into a ball and put into a large bowl sprayed with non-stick spray, cover with a towel; let rise in a warm place until double in size, about 1 hour.

Preheat oven to 400° F. Grease 2 large cookie sheets. Punch dough down, cut in half and place on a floured surface. With a flour-dusted rolling pin, roll dough into 2 12-inch circles. Now you can place toppings onto dough.

Shrimp Adobo

Alaskan spotted shrimp are so tasty, try them in this classic recipe.

Ingredients

2 pounds shrimp (cleaned and peeled)
½ cup soy sauce
1/8 cup vinegar
3 garlic cloves, smashed
8- to 10 whole peppercorns
1 tablespoon vegetable oil
1- to 1½ cups water

Preparation

Sauté shrimp in Dutch oven with vegetable oil, then drain if needed.

Add soy sauce, vinegar, garlic, peppercorns and water; simmer until shrimp are tender. Add water if needed. It should be very saucy.

Optional: Add 1 can coconut milk and 3 dried Thai peppers; both recipes are wonderful, the coconut adds another level of flavor, and peppers a nice heat.

Chapter 8
Delightful Desserts
and Baked Goods
K. Bustillos

Candied Fireweed Flowers

This is a great way to preserve and enjoy our prolific fireweed. They look beautiful on a white frosted cake!

Ingredients:

Fireweed flowers, as many as you can stand to pick and want to make
1 egg white, slightly beaten
1 small paint brush, medium bristle
Sugar, finely ground

Preparation:

Working on paper towels, paint each flower with egg white to dampen. Make sure you dampen but do not saturate. Sprinkle the sugar all around the flower. Let dry completely, about 48 hours. Store in a paper towel-lined, air-tight container for about 3 months.

Baked Apples 

Apples have a long shelf life. You can count on good apples even when we've had an especially long cold snap and the produce section looks quite grim.

Ingredients:

For baked apples, I recommend the Rome Beauty, Braeburn, Gala, or Gravenstein varieties.

4 large apples, washed and cored (do not peel)
¼ cup raisins (soak in warm water for about 20 minutes, then drain well)
¼ cup walnuts, chopped small and coarsely
¼ cup sugar
½ teaspoon cinnamon
¼ cup butter (softened)
Foil sheets

Preheat oven to 350° F.

Preparation:

Mix all the ingredients together in a bowl, except the apples. Stuff all the ingredients into the core opening; wrap up each in a foil sheet. Put onto a cookie sheet; bake for 1 hour or until fork tender.

Optional serving suggestion: Scoop of ice cream or dollop of whipped cream

Suggested Wine:

Gewürztraminer (off dry)

Blueberry Ambrosia

Low bush cranberries also work well for this recipe, if you can find enough of them, that is. This molded salad is our special holiday dish. Violet Reddington sure got a kick out of it when I made it for her 80th birthday party. It was as purple as her outfit!

Ingredients:

2 cups fresh or frozen blueberries, coarsely ground or chopped
1 cup sugar
1 can mandarin oranges, well drained (reserve liquid)
1 can pineapple chunks, well drained (reserve liquid)
1 cup shredded coconut
1 large banana, cubed
2 envelopes unflavored gelatin
1 cup sour cream
1 cup heavy cream

Preparation:

Combine berries and sugar; mix thoroughly to dissolve sugar. Drain oranges and pineapple well, and reserve liquid. Add oranges, pineapple, coconut, and banana to berries. Sprinkle gelatin over ¾ cup of the combined juices to soften. Place over medium heat, stirring constantly to dissolve gelatin; add to fruit mixture. Fold in the sour cream. Whip the heavy cream into stiff peaks; fold into the fruit mixture. Pour mixture into a 13 x 9 x 2-inch pan or 2-quart mold. Chill thoroughly until firm.

When ambrosia is set, dip bottom of mold into a pan of warm water for 30 seconds, put a plate on top, then turn over. It should come out; if not, repeat process.

Suggested Wine:

Fruit wine or Champagne

Honey Corn Bread Muffins

I use Alaskan Fireweed honey in the muffins and whipped honey butter.

Ingredients:

3 cups flour
1 cup cornmeal
¼ cup sugar
2 tablespoons baking powder
2 teaspoons salt
2 sticks (1 cup) butter, melted
3 eggs
2 cups milk
3 tablespoons honey

Preheat oven to 350° F.

Preparation:

Mix together: flour, cornmeal, sugar, baking powder and salt. In a separate bowl, mix together eggs, milk and honey; slowly adding melted butter. Pour into dry ingredients; mix well. Let mixture sit at room temperature for 15 minutes. Pour into prepared muffin pans (sprayed with non-stick spray), bake for approximately 20–25 minutes. Check for doneness.

Honey Butter

½ cup butter, room temperature
4 tablespoons honey

Mix together and serve.

Fresh Apple Pie Muffins

This muffin recipe is fantastic in Alaska even in the coldest of winters. When the produce section of the local grocery store starts looking pretty sparse, you can usually find good apples. Use your favorite apples in this recipe; if you like tart, use tart; if you like sweet, use sweet, or a mixture of the different types.

Ingredients:

3 cups all purpose flour
1 cup sugar
1 cup brown sugar
1 teaspoon baking soda
1 teaspoon salt
1 cup canola oil
½ teaspoon vanilla
3 large eggs
½ teaspoon cinnamon

Mix all these together, and then add the following:

3 cups peeled and chopped apples, about ⅓-inch chunks
½ cup raisins (optional)
½ cup walnuts, chopped (optional)

Preheat oven to 350°F.

Preparation:

Spray or grease muffin pans. This recipe makes 10-12 muffins.

Fill muffin cups about ¾ full. Bake for about 30 minutes. Keep a good eye on them so you don't overcook them.

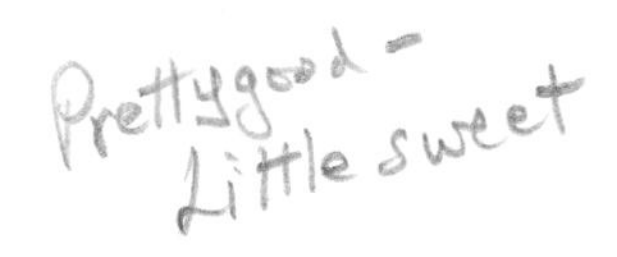

Rhubarb-Peach Crisp

The sweetness of peaches is a great counterbalance to the tartness of rhubarb. With this recipe you get a bonus recipe for rhubarb iced tea.

Ingredients:

Approximately 6 10-inch stalks red rhubarb, peeled and sliced into ½-inch pieces (making sure to peel them first)
4 cups water
1 cup sugar
½ cup sugar (separate)
2 tablespoons flour
2 cups peaches, peeled and sliced (canned or fresh)
Crisp topping – Recipe follows

Preparation:

In a medium sauce pan, add the water and 1 cup sugar; bring to a gentle boil, stirring to melt the sugar. Add the rhubarb slices and cook for 5 minutes. Ladle out the cooked rhubarb, keeping the juice in the pan.

Preheat oven to 350° F.

In a buttered 8 x 8-inch baking dish, put in the cooked rhubarb and peaches. Add the ½ cup sugar and flour, tossing gently. Top with the crisp topping, and bake for approximately 40 minutes or until crispy on top and slightly bubbly.

Crisp Topping

1 stick (¼ pound) butter at room temperature
1 cup flour -try whole wheat flour
½ cup sugar - RAW or BROWN

Mix together into crumbles (best done with clean fingers). Crumble over the fruit.

For more texture, you can add some of the following:

½ cup quick cooking oatmeal
⅓ cup sliced roasted almonds

Suggested Wine:

Muscat/moscato.

Bonus Recipe

Rhubarb Iced Tea

Delicious, refreshing, and full of vitamins.

Take the liquid rhubarb syrup water, taste to adjust strength. Add a little water if it's too strong. Simply pour over ice and presto, great iced tea!!

Birch Syrup Lace Cookies

The dough can last for up to a week in the refrigerator, so only bake the amount of cookies that you will need as the cookies will not keep. Thin, light, and crispy, they go really well with ice cream.

Ingredients:

4 tablespoons unsalted butter
¼ cup birch syrup
¼ cup brown sugar
⅓ cup + 1 tablespoon sifted flour

Preheat oven to 350° F.

Preparation:

In a medium bowl using a hand mixer, beat together the butter, brown sugar, and birch syrup. Gently stir in the flour, mixing only until incorporated. Cover bowl with plastic wrap, pressing all the way down to the dough; you want it air tight. Refrigerate for at least 3 hours, maximum 1 week.

Break off a small piece of dough, about the size of a cherry, rolling dough in your palms to form a small ball. Place on an ungreased cookie sheet about 2 inches apart.

Bake for 7 minutes, or until the cookies spread and look like a golden-colored honeycomb. Remove from the oven, and let them cool for 1 minute. Using a metal spatula, lift from the edge, then push the spatula beneath the cookie with a quick push. If the cookies are sticking to the pan, put them back into the oven for 1 minute to soften up again.

Zucchini Bread

Another great way to use up the large zucchinis we have here in Alaska! The lemon zest adds the secret zing that boosts the flavor.

Ingredients:

3 cups flour
1½ cups sugar
1¼ cups walnuts, chopped
4 teaspoons baking powder
1 teaspoon salt
4 eggs
⅔ cup vegetable oil
2¼ cups zucchini, grated
2 teaspoons lemon zest (grated lemon peel)

Preheat oven to 350° F.

Preparation:

Grease two 8½ x 4½-inch loaf pans. In a large bowl, mix flour, sugar, walnuts, baking powder, and salt. In a medium bowl, beat eggs slightly; stir in oil, zucchini, and lemon peel. Stir the liquid mixture into the dry ingredients, just until the flour is moistened; do not overmix—it will become tough. Divide evenly between the two pans. Bake for 1 hour. Cool in the pans for at least 10 minutes, and then remove breads from the pans.

Blueberry Bread Pudding

A comfort food that can be either sweet or savory. A savory version can be used as a wonderful meal. So many different countries have their own way to use up leftover bread: dishes like stratta (p. 77) or cafoutti. It's all slightly stale bread and a custard; you add the flavors or ingredients that you like. Here I give you a couple of examples.

Ingredients:

1 small round loaf, sliced ¼-inch thick, about 3-inch wide pieces (let it sit out overnight, or use slightly stale).
½ stick butter at room temperture
4 eggs
1 cup ricotta cheese, approximately 8 ounces
1 cup heavy cream
1¼ cups milk
¾ cup sugar
¼ teaspoon cinnamon
¼ teaspoon nutmeg
1 cup blueberries

Preparation:

Preheat oven to 350° F.

In a large bowl, whip eggs; add ricotta, sugar, cinnamon, and nutmeg, stir until smooth. Add cream and milk; mix until well blended.

Butter a 9 x 9 x 3-inch baking dish or souffle dish. Spread butter onto each slice of bread; place one layer into dish, sprinkle with blueberries; repeat until almost to the top of the dish. Pour egg mixture over the layered bread and blueberries; let it sit for 10 minutes. Cover loosely with foil; bake for 40 minutes, uncover and continue baking for 20 minutes more until golden brown.

Variations:

Apple Cinnamon Bread Pudding—same except add 2 cups sliced apples instead of blueberries. Increase cinnamon to 1 teaspoon.

Pate Choux (paht-ah-shoo)
Puff Pastry

I use these puffs for appetizers, crème puffs or éclairs. These are easy to make and great to eat. Here is my recipe for this classic pastry and ideas on great uses!

Ingredients:

½ cup butter (1 stick)
½ cup water
¼ teaspoon salt
1 cup flour
4 eggs

Preparation:

Preheat oven to 350°F. Grease 2 cookie sheets.

In a 2-quart saucepan, heat butter and water until boiling. Turn off heat, add flour all at once. Stir in well. The dough should come away from the sides of the pan. Remove the pan from the stove and stir in the eggs, one at a time until fully incorporated. Use a greased scooper (use the size scoop for the size puff you want) to make balls on cookie sheets. For desserts, I make them medium or large.

How long you cook them depends on the size of the puffs. Here is the basic rule: Cook until golden brown, pull them out, and pierce each puff to let the steam escape. Cook 10 minutes longer. Turn off the oven, leaving the puffs in for 10 more minutes–this dries them out a little. Take them out of the oven and let cool.

Cut off the tops; scrape out the little extra dough inside. Fill them with your favorite sweet or savory filling mixture.

Vanilla Pudding

For a sweet idea for stuffing your puffs, you might try a vanilla pudding. This is a very simple recipe but very tasty. Use a very good, real vanilla extract. It makes a big difference in the flavor.

Ingredients:

2 cups milk
1½ teaspoon vanilla extract
3 tablespoons cornstarch
4½ tablespoons sugar
1/8 teaspoon salt

Preparation:

In a 2-quart heavy-bottomed saucepan, mix the cornstarch, sugar, and salt with ¼ cup milk, set aside. In a small saucepan on medium heat, heat the remaining milk just until hot, then slowly add it to the cornstarch mixture, stirring constantly. Cook until thickened, continue cooking for 10 more minutes over a low heat. Now add the vanilla, mix in well, let cool, cover and chill.

Appetizer Suggestion:

For appetizers, I make the puffs small and stuff them with curried chicken, halibut, or salmon salad and top them with fruit chutney. Try these puffs with Curried Halibut Salad (p. 9) and Fruit Chutney from *Suzette's International Cooking* (p. 81).

The End

Food Resources

General information:
Alaska Division of Agriculture
1800 Glenn Hwy, Ste. 12
Palmer, Alaska 99645
907-745-7200
http://dnr.alaska.gov/ag/

Alaska seafood:
New Sagaya International Market
3700 Old Seward Highway
Anchorage, Alaska 99503
907-561-5173
www.newsagaya.com
seafood@newsagaya.com

Alaska game meat:
Indian Valley Meats
200 Huot Circle
Indian, Alaska 99540
907-653-7511
www.indianvalleymeats.com

Alaskan birch syrup:
Kahiltna Birchworks
P.O. Box 2267
Palmer, Alaska 99645
907-373-1309; 1-800-380-7457
www.alaskabirchsyrup.com

Fresh and smoked fowl–eggs–local meat & dairy:
Tripole D Farm and Hatchery
5840 Gershmel Loop
Palmer, Alaska 99645
907-376-3338

For "Rent-A-Chef" services by Suzette Lord Weldon call 907-357-Chef (2433)

ORDER FORM

I would like to order my own or another copy of the book *Suzette's Alaskan Cooking* by Suzette Lord Weldon. Please send me:

books x $19.95 per copy = ______________

+ Postage (first class) & handling @ $4.95/book: ______________

TOTAL ENCLOSED $ ______________

We accept cash, check, or money order made out to Northbooks, or VISA, Mastercard. Prices subject to change without notice.

(You may phone your VISA/MC order to Northbooks at 907-696-8973)

VISA/MC card # | | | | | | | | | | | | | | | | |

Exp. date: ___/___ Amount charged: $ ______________

Signature: ______________________________

Phone number: ____________________

Please send my book (s) to:

Name: ______________________________

Address: ______________________________

City: ____________ State: ________ Zip: __________

Please fill out this order form and send to:

Northbooks

17050 N. Eagle River Loop Rd, #3

Eagle River, AK 99577-7804

(907) 696-8973

www.northbooks.com

LaVergne, TN USA
15 October 2010
200963LV00002B/1/P
9 780981 519364